...we genuinely are connected in a way that makes us kin. We share a majority of the genes that serve as instructions for building and managing our bodies and minds.

Four Fifths a Grizzly

A New Perspective on Nature that Just Might Save Us All

Patagonia publishes a select list of titles on wilderness, wildlife, and outdoor sports that inspire and restore a connection to the natural world.

© 2021 Douglas Chadwick

Photograph/Illustration copyrights held by the photographer/illustrator as indicated in captions.

Hardcover Edition

Printed in the United States on Roland Enviro 100 Satin FSC® certified 100% post-consumer-waste paper.

Editor—John Dutton
Photo Editor—Jane Sievert
Art Director, Designer—Christina Speed
Figures and Maps—Christina Speed
Project Manager—Sonia Moore
Photo Archivist—Taylor Norton, Tee Smith, and Angelo Partemi
Print Production—Rafael Dunn, Michaela Purcilly, and Tausha Greenblott
Publisher—Karla Olson

Hardcover ISBN 978-1-952338-01-4
E-Book ISBN 978-1-952338-02-1
Library of Congress Control Number 2021934264

Published by Patagonia Works

FRONT COVER PHOTOS:
The author and one of his many relatives, a Scandinavian brown bear. JOE RIIS AND MORTEN KOLDBY

FRONT END SHEET PHOTO: *A male drill at a primate rehabilitation center in Nigeria, drills share more than 90 percent of their genes with us.* CYRIL RUOSO/ MINDEN PICTURES

TITLE PAGE PHOTO: *The larva of a small octopus with the sassy scientific name* Wunderpus photogenicus *off the Philippines. What looks like a large brain is a digestive organ. Yet* Wunderpus *does have a central brain there and eight secondary "brains," one for each arm.* WU YUNG-SEN

ENVIRONMENTAL BENEFITS STATEMENT

Patagonia, Inc. saved the following resources by printing the pages of this book on process chlorine free paper made with 100% post-consumer waste versus paper made with virgin fiber.

TREES	WATER	ENERGY	SOLID WASTE	GREENHOUSE GASES
251	20,000	105	800	108,200
FULLY GROWN	GALLONS	MILLION BTUs	POUNDS	POUNDS

Environmental impact estimates were made using the Environmental Paper Network Paper Calculator 4.0. For more information visit www.papercalculator.org.

FSC
www.fsc.org
MIX
Paper from responsible sources
FSC® C002589

1% FOR THE PLANET
MEMBER

Dedication

It only seems right to dedicate this book to Karen, Teal, Russell, Thomas, Gordon, and the rest of my kin, which includes every life form you ever heard of, a lot you probably never heard of, and millions upon millions that nobody knows because they haven't been discovered. Yet.

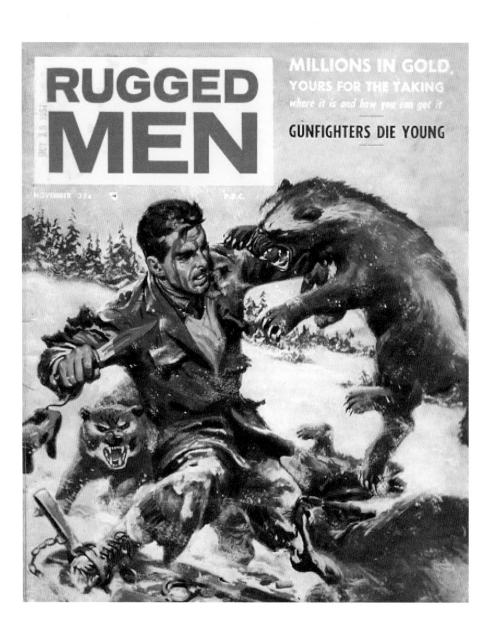

RUGGED MEN

MILLIONS IN GOLD,
YOURS FOR THE TAKING
where it is and how you can get it

GUNFIGHTERS DIE YOUNG

NOVEMBER 35¢

CONTENTS

There are no valid accounts of free-roaming wolverines attacking humans, only instances of a trapped animal trying to defend itself. The only wild thing truly represented in this vintage "man versus nature" scene is the artist's imagination. CRESTWOOD PUBLISHING/ STANLEY PUBLICATIONS/ NORMANDY ASSOCIATES

PROLOGUE

Everything in a natural system is connected. This isn't a platitude. It is the principle that explains how a mineral orb wheeling through the vacuum of space became wrapped in creatures—became a biosphere with mushrooms that glow in the dark, kaleidoscopic dancing spiders, puppies and kittens, six-foot-long salamanders that both bark and mewl, Komodo dragons that reproduce by "virgin births," jellyfish capable of reversing the aging process and existing forever, chimpanzees with nearly 99 percent of the same genes we own making tools in an African woodland, and so many microbes that they outnumber the stars in the known universe. That's life.

Microbes (short for microorganisms, most of which consist of a single cell) produce a critical share of the Earth's oxygen. They permeate the planet's seas. They make weather: wafting through the skies overhead in unseen hordes that seed the formation of clouds. Billions pulse in each handful of the soil under your feet, manufacturing fertility. Trillions flourish in your gut and mouth and on your skin. You host trillions more in the form of ancient bacteria that evolved to become permanent residents inside each of your cells (and those of all other animals and plants), where they generate the chemical energy that powers everything you do—grow, move, feel, learn.

. . .

On the top floor of his three-story family home, a boy sits at a desk in the light from a dormer window. As the eldest child, he was moved upstairs when younger children filled the second-floor bedrooms nearest their parents. At nine years of age—maybe ten now—he is old enough to have kissed a girl's mouth on a dare, yet not so old that, alone in his attic on a windy, creaky night, he can completely ignore the possibility of monsters in the crawl spaces of the eaves.

The boy pitches for the local Little League baseball team. He mows neighborhood lawns and shovels sidewalks for pocket money. He hangs out with buddies in a garage loft clubhouse, joins them in exploring the steep bluffs on the edge of town, loves to blow stuff up with firecrackers, and gets into the occasional bloody-nosed scrap. For the most part, he's a regular, rowdy kid. Yet, as he is doing now, he also spends hours by himself peering through a microscope. It is not from a Junior Scientist kit. This is an old, professional B&L (Bausch & Lomb) model with precisely calibrated lenses encased in finely machined brass. His father, a mining geologist, had used the instrument to examine mineral structures and passed it along as a gift. Each time the boy takes the microscope from its wooden carrying case and sets it out on the dormer desk, where the metal gives off a glow of reflected light, he feels a connection to scientists past and present, the Big League of curiosity experts.

There are three eyepieces of different magnifying power to choose from for placing atop the viewing tube. On a revolving turret at the tube's base are four objective lenses of different strength that multiply the power of the eyepieces. The boy had peered through strong handheld magnifying glasses before, marveling at the oddity of familiar objects like newsprint or the whorls of

A professional Bausch & Lomb microscope from the late 1800s that the author inherited as a child became his magic tunnel opening into whole worlds of life he'd never been aware of before.

grooves and ridges on his own fingertips. But he had no inkling of what something would look like enlarged to 40, 100, or even 400 times normal size. He does now.

. . .

At the start, he rummaged through the house and yard for anything that would fit under the lenses: salt crystals, cat fur, cereal, dirt, a leaf, a scab picked off his knee, beetle antennae. Every familiar material he managed to bring into clear focus proved full of stunning details and promised to reveal more secrets under stronger magnification. When he tried that, though, even thin and fragile-looking objects merely turned into great dark lumps. So the boy crowded reading lamps around the platform, where the glass slide holding a specimen was placed. That helped—up to a point.

Soon, his father was driving him to a scientific supply house to get strong directional microscope lights and stains that brought out certain features of tissues and cells. The boy also brought home slides with a shallow bowl carved out in the center to hold liquids. At last, he could drop pond water on a slide and tour a globule of creation populated by miniscule squirmers and swimmers without them draining away when he moved the glass around.

Almost every day that he put his modest advances in microscope techniques to use, he encountered something entirely new, some form, process, or setting unlike anything he ever saw or could imagine before. This was mind-bending territory. MoldLand: blotches of rot on bread, cheese, or fruit transformed into storybook forests; lollipop trees that seemed built from beads in one sample, a tangled filament jungle in the next. PollenLand:

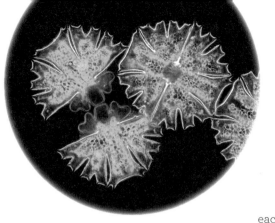

a smear of powder resolved into a galaxy of fertile sun-colored spheres, each with a perfect geometric pattern of golf ball–like dimples or urchin-like spikes—or both. BloodLand: the dab from a pricked finger became a flotilla of little round corpuscles—scarlet cells that looked like life rafts sliding past one another inside a slowly congealing swirl of organic magma. Often, the boy found himself holding watch over multitudes of different life forms at once within a fresh sample of water as they lashed, spun, squiggled, throbbed, and sometimes budded or pinched off spores or pumped out tiny eggs.

In particular, I—sure, I was this kid—remember my first success at keeping the semi-transparent wanderings of an amoeba in view at high power for a while. That single-celled organism brushed up against a smaller one and slowly, relentlessly, enveloped it. I watched the captive swimming through the protoplasm of its captor until the amoeba dissolved the creature's outer membrane and absorbed the streaming broth inside, turning everything that had been a separate existence into more oozing amoeba. Not long afterward, this predator twinned by slowly dividing itself into two roughly equal blobs. AmoebaLand: where it couldn't be more clear that you are what you eat.

Micrasterias (meaning little star), a single-celled algae. Though able to carry out photosynthesis, it is not a plant but a member of the huge and varied group of single-celled life forms called protists.
FRANK FOX/
SCIENCE SOURCE

The disc-like human red blood cells raft through the circulatory system carrying oxygen from the lungs to the body's other cells. Their color comes from the iron-rich protein hemoglobin, which binds to the oxygen.
AUREL MANEA

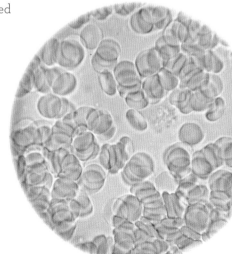

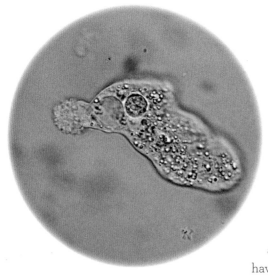

The term amoeba includes thousands of single-celled species with a variety of sizes, shapes, and lifestyles. This is a fairly typical type, which moves by extending a pseudopod (false foot) and oozing in that direction. JAN VAN ARKEL/MINDEN PICTURES

After pulling my eye away from the B&L, I puzzled over whether amoebas today might be descended unchanged from the very first one on the planet or possibly were that first one, which had been feeding and splitting through the ages. Many replicates must have died, but many lived to divide and copy themselves again and again. Could an amoeba be sort of immortal in this way? What were the amoebocytes that our household encyclopedia described roaming the bodies of a variety of larger animals? The encyclopedia said they distributed food or got rid of wastes in some species, changed into different types of cells to build structures in other organisms, and protected many more by attacking harmful microbes. And what gave rise to the amoeba-like type of white blood cells that defend the human body by engulfing and devouring infectious "germs"?

Like the creatures I observed, my questions grew and took on different forms and proliferated. Although I was pretty sure that real scientists had worked out the answers, I didn't know how to look them up in professional journals and couldn't make a whole lot of sense of the few technical explanations I did manage to find. But I liked trying. My usual concerns still ranged from trading comic books to raiding leftover dessert from the fridge before my brothers got to it, yet when the brass B&L stood lamp-lit and ready, I would travel again to unexpected realms and uncover more "lands" and more questions.

In retrospect, the best thing about those boyhood hours at the microscope is that they were powered purely by fascination. I never felt obligated to do what I was doing. I never had a purpose. And, as a pre-preteen, I was too young to care whether anybody thought spending so much time staring at mega-magnified stuff was geeky. My notions of what actually existed around, underfoot, and inside me were getting reconstructed as I began to absorb a core fact about life on Earth: most of it is invisible.

Through nearly all of human history, nobody understood the real scope of nature, simply because no one suspected that the vast majority and greatest variety of organisms sharing the world couldn't be seen with normal vision. But the B&L Kid had his magical gadget, and with it experienced the astonishment felt by the first people to ever peer through microscopes three centuries earlier. His world changed. The smaller the scale of lives and activities the boy looked at through the lenses, the more alive they made the everyday settings that hold them all seem.

. . .

By the time I reached my early twenties, I was still propelled by this yearning to focus on nature and stay amazed. But I was ready to try doing it from a fresh vantage point. I'd always been drawn to books about naturalist-explorers, fossil-hunters, anthropologists, mountain-climbers, cavers, and just about anybody else whose career mixed adventure and discovery. I loved hiking and camping and dreamed all through my high school and undergraduate years of being able to spend more days roaming the outdoors. Way more days, and way farther outdoors. And now the B&L sat in storage while I looked through the lenses of binoculars instead, studying mountain goats in the soaring upper reaches of Montana's Rockies.

Sharp-horned, shaggy, snow-white, and more closely related to musk oxen than to true goats, these master climbers dwell higher and steeper year-round than any other large mammal in North America. Not a great deal was known about their natural history. To learn about it in detail, I spent seven years following herds along the crown of the continent. It was hard, cliffy, often risky going, especially through the winters. But the settings were wild and powerfully beautiful, and I had never felt so free.

Mountain goats (like this one shedding old winter fur) dwell higher and steeper year-round than any other hoofed animal in North America. The author studied them atop the Rocky Mountains for seven years. Glacier National Park, Montana.
STEVEN GNAM

What was the best way to survive among those peaks? The longer I stayed there watching mountain goats and their neighbors—dusky grouse, elk, wolverines, hoary marmots, nighthawks, cutthroat trout, and grizzly bears—the more I came to see how each species' physical traits and behaviors combined to form the right answer for that question. I experienced the same sense of being privy to wonders that I'd had while looking at creatures through a microscope. I just needed to shoulder a heavy pack and cover a lot more ground to keep my current subjects in view.

Throughout this period, geneticists and molecular biologists using new laboratory technologies were uncovering more and more evidence of pervasive bonds between humans and other life forms, including the thousands of different species dwelling inside each person's body and influencing its workings at almost every level. But the scientists' breakthroughs weren't what first led me to see the human world and the natural world as indivisible. Months-long spells of living out of a tent or in a little open space under a tarpaulin strung between trees, contending

FOUR FIFTHS A GRIZZLY

with the same weather and seasonal changes as every animal and plant around me, did that.

Yet other forces intruded on the backcountry in the meantime. Each year, newly bulldozed roads brought vehicles, heavy equipment, logging operations, fossil fuel exploration, and hunting pressures farther into what had been remote strongholds for the native flora and fauna. The combination was proving too much for the mountain goats, which, like the trees at upper elevations, grow and reproduce slowly in their extreme environment. The herds were in widespread decline. Grizzly bears were in worse trouble, having been pared down to less than 2 percent of their former range and numbers south of Canada. Together with findings from researchers elsewhere, the data I gathered helped spur wildlife managers to scale back hunting pressure on the goats. I also played a minor role in gaining protection for the grizzlies under the Endangered Species Act. Once I wrapped up my research in the Rockies, it was time to look into other possibilities. But can you picture the job opportunities awaiting someone whose sole entry under experience on a job application is "high-altitude goatboy"? No? Me neither.

Because I was still fired up about the rate at which wildlife and wild places were dwindling, I found myself writing on this subject to let the public know more about what was going on out there. My articles were mostly for nonprofit conservation publications. They paid so little that my writing career was pretty much nonprofit too. This was a non-problem, though, because Karen Reeves kept food on the table. During summer, she worked as the fire guard at a mountaintop lookout tower. In the cold months, she tended bar at the one saloon in the setting where we lived—a sixty-mile-long river valley running between two ranges

FOUR FIFTHS A GRIZZLY

of peaks. Lacking utilities and serviced by a two-lane dirt road, the area was also home to the lower forty-eight states' densest remaining population of grizzly bears. Karen would watch them for hours on end in the bottomland meadows each spring.

You're darn right I married Karen. Eventually I also lucked into paid assignments from *National Geographic* magazine and other popular publications to report on the natural realm, often in distant parts of the world. Whenever I returned to western North America, I kept going out to watch grizzlies in my spare time. I didn't think much about why. Although I hoped to understand more about their behavior and the obstacles to their survival, the main draw for me was witnessing their indomitably wild spirit—one that, after more than a century of persecution, still reared up to say the hell with you two-leggeds and your whole tamed-down, fenced-in, crowded-up version of progress.

. . .

Wherever I went around the globe, human populations were growing and spreading like a flood tide. Around the time of Christ, Earth had perhaps 300 million people and scattered environmental problems. Today, we total close to 8 billion and face an entire biosphere in crisis. Reliable indicators point toward a much greater share of the planet's species and resulting biological stability vanishing before the current century is out, quite possibly derailing our own future. This destructive pattern probably won't change until we change the way we think about our relationship to nature.

All of us want to one day make sense of life in a way that will deliver answers to the BIG questions: Who am I? Where am I going? What does it all mean?

VOL. 193, NO. 3 · MARCH 1998

NATIONAL GEOGRAPHIC

Planet of the beetles 100

MARINE SANCTUARIES 2
NAPLES UNABASHED 32
THE RISE OF LIFE ON EARTH 54
AMERICA'S FIRST HIGHWAY 82
NOMADS OF THE ARCTIC 120

OFFICIAL JOURNAL OF THE NATIONAL GEOGRAPHIC SOCIETY WASHINGTON, D.C.

A good start toward answering the first question would be for people to better understand the microbial, genetic, and behavioral connections we already have with the living world. These natural qualities define who we are; both human and considerably more than that. Drawing from advances in the scientific knowledge of recent decades and from my own experiences, I want to illuminate what goes into the making of our greater selves.

My other goal in this book is to address the question a lot of us ask almost daily when faced with the endless discouraging news about what's happening to the global environment and our fellow Earthlings. What can any one person do right now that's going to make a meaningful difference?

The answer is: Plenty. Among the later chapters, you'll find examples of helpful changes individuals can make in their own lives. You'll also find descriptions of large-scale, transformative conservation plans that are hands-on practical, well underway, and proving to be the kinds of models for success anyone might be motivated to draw from.

While most chapters can be read as stand-alone essays, they are arranged to build upon one another. The nature of nature is a huge subject. This book is by no means intended to cover every base. It is meant to blend fresh information and ideas together with the kind of hope we need to keep us company on a new path guided by an adapted golden rule: Do unto ecosystems as you would have them do unto you.

Nurture, sustain health, allow to flourish.

Over the years since I took up writing, I sought out more places where I could keep grizzlies in view. These bears have always been particularly good at helping me figure out when to stay quiet and watch carefully, and when you'd better make some noise and get ready to move.

Like NOW.

NEXT SPREAD

Harsh drought conditions force Tanzania's hippos to congregate in the Katavi National Park, where they churned shrinking pools into mud baths. MICHAEL POLIZA

Hot weather in Suining, in China's Sichuan province, can turn public swimming pools into near-solid stews of humans buoyed by flotation rings. ZHONG MIN/ VISUAL CHINA GROUP/GETTY IMAGES

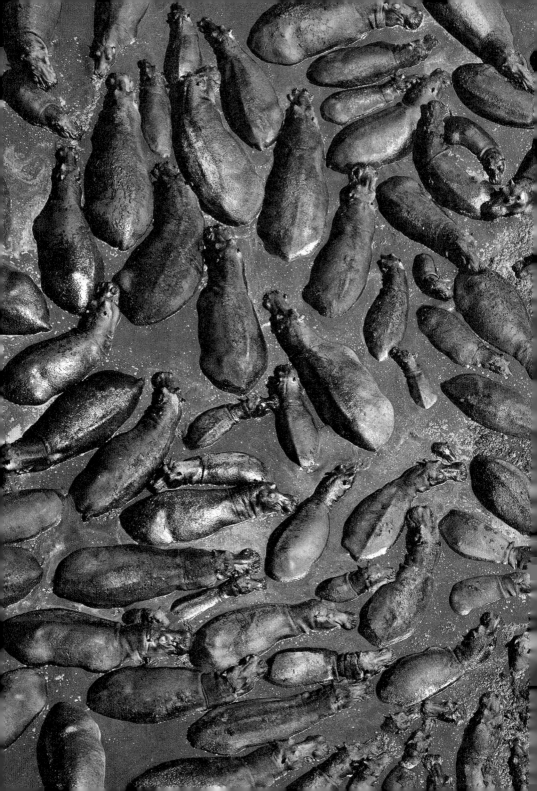

I'm at Least Four-Fifths Grizzly Bear

On a warm day in May along the southern coast of British Columbia, I paddled my kayak into the tidal estuary at the head of a small bay where I'd been many times before. Icefields patterned the mountain horizon behind me. Ahead, thick rainforest enclosed the estuary and its islands of silt topped with grass-like sedges. Rounding the bend in a narrow channel, I heard a Canada goose on shore start muttering about something. I steered closer to find out what was going on. Turned out I didn't need to be closer to see a full-grown grizzly stand up from among the green stalks maybe twenty yards away.

I know; this sounds like the opening of a bear encounter drama. But no, I backpaddled slowly and as quietly as I could and tripled the distance between us. The grizz never looked my way. It tilted its nose up to sample breezes coming from the opposite direction and then dropped smoothly down onto all fours to graze the new sedge growth. Every once in a while, the animal raised its broad head to glance briefly in the direction of the breeze. Otherwise, it fed continuously.

Grizzlies, also called brown bears, belong to the species *Ursus arctos*, and were originally found across most of the Northern Hemisphere. Of all the stories told of the mighty grizz

When a person comes eye to eye with a grizzly bear, a lot of what happens next can depend upon what each knows about the other. NEIL EVER OSBORNE

CHAPTER ONE

through the years, you've never heard or read about one being boring, right? But go for a look in spring when the upsurge of nutrients stored in roots over winter makes some plants' tender new shoots nearly as rich in protein as meat. Wherever you come upon a grizzly in green-up time, that animal is likely to be grazing—and to keep on grazing until you begin to wonder if somebody didn't throw a bear hide over a cow.

Half a dozen Canada geese were plucking new sedge shoots not far from the bear. When it swung its head and stepped toward the birds to reach a new clump of sedge, they reacted with a few honks and half-raised wings but soon returned to eating. The only thing remotely in danger of dying was my butt, growing short of blood as I waited motionless on the hard kayak seat while the minutes ticked by. All at once, the geese took noisy flight. Two yearling cubs appeared moments later at the large bear's side. They were what she had been checking on. The cubs must have been resting or nearby; I was too low in the water to have seen them behind the taller sedges. When the family moved closer to where the main stream running through the estuary pours into the bay, I paddled back out into the open water. There, I could scoot around watching at enough of a distance that I wouldn't have to worry about disturbing anyfurrybody.

After a while, another bear stepped out of the forest. It waded through a channel and kept moving toward the bear family. Although close to the mother's height, the intruder had the slender, rangy look of a subadult maybe four years old. It seemed as though this bear and the female were somewhat familiar with each other, for she showed little reaction as it came closer. The subadult was twenty yards away before the mother stiffened. After stepping closer together, they turned at the same time and

Grizzly females may have as many as four cubs, but the most common number is two, like this clingy pair in Lake Clark National Park and Preserve, Alaska.
PETER DERRINGTON

began walking parallel to one another—until the mother made a lunge. As far as I know, nobody is allowed to get close to a female grizzly's cubs except, rarely, one of her offspring from a previous year. The other bear wheeled and bolted, and the mother started after it.

Storybook bears are often depicted as being on the bumbly, pot-bellied end of the animal athlete spectrum. Grizz do get portly in zoos, which is where most people see them nowadays. In the wild, you're not likely to find chubby bears until autumn, when they need to pack on enough fat to keep them alive for the months they will be in winter dens. Even layered with lard, a grizzly's thick underlying musculature gives it quick reflexes and remarkable agility to go with its brute strength. Within a couple eyeblinks, the subadult was in full flight with the mother close on its heels, and both heavy animals were powering along at least as fast as the local deer, whose top speed is more than thirty miles per hour.

Mom finally put on the brakes. Moments later, one of the cubs caught up with her and went galloping on ahead as if determined to catch the intruder, despite being maybe a quarter the subadult's size. I had the sense that the cub was putting on a brave show—That's right, Dipstick, you better keep on runnin' from Fearsome Junior Bear—because it kept looking back over its shoulder as if to double-check that Mom was still nearby.

An hour later, the mother lay in the sun on an open bank, stretching, scratching, tinkering a while with a little driftwood chunk she held between her paws. Close behind her, the cubs stood with their paws on each other's shoulders, wrestling like dancers. A different female with young had arrived on the other side of the estuary. While she grazed, her new little cubs—recently

emerged from their sunless birth den into a world full of scents and motion—raced up tilted driftwood logs and splashed through the shallows chasing gulls at the edge of the retreating tide. It's good to be a grizzly bear on a wild shore of the sea. And it's good to be a grizzly bear–watcher being watched in turn by curious harbor seals whose big-eyed heads pop up next to the kayak now and then.

Although they amble at a leisurely pace, grizzlies can go from a standstill to a thirty-five-mile-per-hour sprint in seconds. This young coastal bear is merely escaping a sibling during a play chase.
IAN MCALLISTER

. . .

I don't claim to know how grizzly bears think. But this seldom stops me from trying to imagine what the bear I have in sight is going to do in a given situation and then compare that with what the bear actually does. I take delight in occasionally not being wrong. As evidence of bear worship by prehistoric people—not to mention countless children's books and stuffed teddy bears—affirm, an inclination to identify with *Ursus* is hardly unusual. They are genuinely much like us in a number of ways.

Being omnivores with high energy requirements, they eat just about every type of food we do: new green vegetation; the roots, bulbs, berries, and nuts where plant nutrients become concentrated; honey (of course); fish; eggs; and animals of all sizes. Counting insects and scavenged meat, I can't think offhand of anything grizzlies consume that modern humans and their ancestors haven't also made meals of. The bears have the very relatable habit of standing and occasionally moving around on two legs, and they use their paws and long-clawed toes with surprising dexterity. At times, they also give the impression of mulling things over before they act.

An assortment of other animals such as ravens, dolphins, elephants, and nonhuman primates show obvious learning talents and have been observed solving problems both in captivity and in the wild. Grizzly bears have one of the largest brains relative to body size among land-dwelling carnivores. They keep adding to the information their gray matter stores, learning and recalling settings in which they found abundant food, experienced danger, and so on throughout a life span of thirty years or more. So if it looks to you that the bear you have a close eye on just paused as if considering its options, that's probably what it was doing, though how much any grizz version of thought resembles ours is a wild guess.

With these bears' intelligence comes a marked curiosity. They seem scarcely able to resist investigating things and

Contemporary Inuvialuit sculptor David Ruben Piqtoukun calls this figure "Bear in Shamanic Transformation."
ARTWORK: DAVID RUBEN
IMAGE: RANDY DODSON/FINE ARTS MUSEUM SAN FRANCISCO

manipulating objects, one more reason for humans to empathize with the bear persona. As lords of the landscape, grizzlies can indulge their inquisitiveness with little risk of harm from another kind of animal. Being dominant within the wildlife community also allows them to take part in longer sessions of play than more vulnerable creatures can afford as a rule. Even a solitary bear crossing a meadow may suddenly break into a trot, leap toward the ground, tuck its head, and turn the dive into a somersault, then get up and do it all over again. And again. The convergence of dominance, inquisitiveness, and playfulness certainly applies to humans as well. It also comes to the fore in two other top-ranking mammals I've watched here, the coastal wolf packs that visit the estuary and the killer whale groups that occasionally sweep into the bay.

Your awareness of another grizzly trait, the potential for the kind of aggression

that could leave you in shreds, never completely goes away when you're observing these bears in their natural habitats. Yet the same concern keeps you paying attention more intently than you would with most species. And that makes you better at catching subtle expressions, postures, and momentary hesitations, and better at reading between the bold lines of a bear's actions. Sooner or later, you feel that you're beginning to break through the boundary of "otherness" between you and the bear—past the old stories; past the statistics about reproduction, diet, habitat preferences, etc., and into the essence of a similar savvy, emotional being.

· · ·

I realize now that it's really been a combination of three elements that have drawn me to watch grizzlies for hundreds of hours over the years. The first is that where these great mammals still roam, the land is most likely to have stayed wild and remain home to all the other native species that belong there. In other words, roaming grizzly country is a special joy whether I see bears or not. Second ... alright, I am sort of an adrenaline junkie. Not that I don't work hard to keep a sensible distance from grizz, but being anywhere within sight of them makes me feel alive in all the ways we and our ancestors were designed to survive in environments with a full complement of Big Bite-You's. Being pumped up in all five senses and whatever that ineffable sixth sense tingling underneath them is—that's really what I'm addicted to. The third element is the connection I feel when once again watching these fellow mammals long enough to see them not as anything I feared or hoped or was told they were but just as grizzly bears being grizzly bears. Which ends up being a whole lot more fascinating.

I'm aware that this sense of connection is in my imagination and that the bears don't give a grizzled goddamn what I think. But I know something they don't, which is that we genuinely are connected in a way that makes us kin. We share a majority of the genes that serve as instructions for building and managing our bodies and minds. While enough grizzly bear gene sequences have been identified to allow comparisons with other bear species, I haven't come across a direct comparison with humans yet. However, a more complete genetic analysis has been done for an assortment of other mammals. We know, for instance, that dogs share 84 percent of their genes with us, and cattle share 85 percent. Ordinary mice share a surprising 85 percent. One of the many hunters of mice, the domestic Abyssinian cat, shares 90 percent. So it's fairly safe to assume that we and grizzly bears have somewhere between 80 and 90 percent of our genes in common.

Chimpanzees and the closely related bonobos possess at least 97 percent of the same genes we do. When strictly comparing only genes and not the exact sequences in which they appear along a chromosome, the figure rises to almost 99 percent according to some calculations. During an expedition to survey wildlife in the swampy rainforest headwaters of the Congo River, I encountered a group of fifteen or more chimps that had never seen a human before. Living in an area filled with other chimpanzee bands, lowland gorillas, and a dozen different species of monkeys might have made the troop that visited us all the more curious about what our kinda-sorta-similar-looking troop of half-naked Caucasians and Aka Pygmies might be. As the chimps gradually edged closer both on the ground and in overhanging tree branches, they took their eyes off us only to cast quick glances at their companions, as if one of them might have an answer.

Mike Fay, the explorer I was with, told me how chimpanzees in this region not only fashion twigs into tools for poking into termite mounds and extracting some of the colonies' members to snack on, but also carry around digging sticks for probing the forest soil in search of insect larvae. In addition, they use large pieces of wood to club open the mud nests of bees to get honey. Now and then, we could hear the chimps communicating over a distance using their version of jungle drums—the fin-like buttresses that flare out from the base of certain tropical trees to provide extra support. Large and thin, these panes of wood reverberate like sounding boards when struck, amplifying the drumming. Although there may be a couple percent difference in our genomes, what I remember most about those animals is their boldly inquisitive gaze. Calculating one moment, wide with astonishment the next, it felt 100 percent human.

If I were to walk up to folks on the street and give them the news that the DNA in each of their cells is 80 to 90 percent identical to a grizzly bear's, I doubt I'd be taken seriously, much less welcomed to stick around. I guess I wouldn't blame them, especially since when people hear the word grizzly, many call up the image of some towering ton of gut-crunching terror they saw in a movie or on a TV show. But the number of genes we share with a grizzly obviously doesn't mean that we look and act 80 to 90 percent like even a realistic-size one. Every mammal needs to regulate cell metabolism, oxidize sugars, generate electrical impulses, coordinate packets of muscles, blink, chew, move, make milk, filter waste products, fight off pathogens, get plenty of warm blood to the brain, and we all do it with the same molecular tools. Even the egg-laying, duck-billed, barely-a-mammal platypus shares about 82 percent of its genes with us. As for other

A young female chimpanzee in Tanzania's Gombe National Park fishes for termites with a plant stalk. First observed in her kind, tool use has since been described for a number of other wild mammals and birds. ANUP SHAH/ NATUREPL

CHAPTER ONE

I'M AT LEAST FOUR-FIFTHS GRIZZLY BEAR

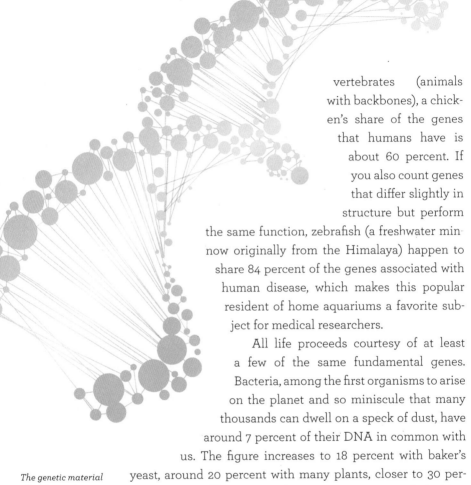

vertebrates (animals with backbones), a chicken's share of the genes that humans have is about 60 percent. If you also count genes that differ slightly in structure but perform the same function, zebrafish (a freshwater minnow originally from the Himalaya) happen to share 84 percent of the genes associated with human disease, which makes this popular resident of home aquariums a favorite subject for medical researchers.

All life proceeds courtesy of at least a few of the same fundamental genes. Bacteria, among the first organisms to arise on the planet and so miniscule that many thousands can dwell on a speck of dust, have around 7 percent of their DNA in common with us. The figure increases to 18 percent with baker's yeast, around 20 percent with many plants, closer to 30 percent with rice and bananas, and 40 percent or more with the likes of honeybees and fruit flies. Again, such numbers vary somewhat from one report to another depending on what is being compared, for genes may become part of different sequences from species to species or occupy quite different locations on a chromosome strand.

Here's how I think about it: However broadly or narrowly one defines identical genes, I am in a sense alive in a mind-boggling

The genetic material of most organisms consists of DNA molecules in which two long chains of nucleotide molecules form a double helix linked by chemical bonds. Within that dual spiral is stored the code for life.

CHAPTER ONE

number of creatures in a staggering range of environments around the globe through the DNA we share. I leap, I fly, I slither. I shimmer with iridescent scales in the waters off Zanzibar, and I stretch my petals toward the light in far northern Siberia. Being more closely related to avocados, ants, and aardvarks than most people suspect doesn't dilute our stature as humans but instead increases it manyfold. It renders us more than human. This is our deep heritage, an old, enduring kinship as big as the living world.

Molecular analyses of genomes and the mathematics involved make the subject sound theoretical. The grizz at the estuary—and in the mountains around my Montana home—make it solid and exciting. Like every creature, grizz are more than fellow Earthlings. They are our greater selves. I realize now that what mostly drew me to the bears from the start is that I get

All life proceeds courtesy of at least a few of the same fundamental genes.

keyed up enough in their presence to be able to see and sense myself in them and them in me.

Scientists have classified about 1.5 million species so far and expect to find millions more. More than two-thirds of those known species are insects. Thus far, entomologists have named some 400,000 different kinds of beetles alone, and it looks as though most of the organisms awaiting discovery will prove to be more insects, other invertebrates, and a very long list of microbes. All the vertebrates in existence—the fish, amphibians, reptiles, birds, and mammals—add up to roughly 66,000 species. It's a strikingly small group as major divisions of organisms go. But these animals had an outsize role in shaping our hominid ancestors' reflexes, instincts, and skills over millions of years. Modern humans, *Homo sapiens*, arose as early as 350,000 years ago, and for nearly all the years since then, the vertebrates, and especially other mammals, continued to be a major influence on our activities and characteristics, including the thoughts, stories, art, and prayers of people's cultures.

According to a 2018 summary in the *Journal of Mammalogy*, the exact species count for present-day mammals came to 6,495. However, ninety-six appear to have gone missing (extinct) lately, so let's round off the total at 6,400. Estimates for the number of species of all kinds existing on Earth today, including all the mostly microscopic forms yet to be discovered, range from 8 million to as many as 100 million. If we pick, say, 10 million as the actual number to be on the conservative side, the mammals add up to just .005 of 1 percent of the total. That's it in the way of warm-blooded, haired, milk-producing beings on this planet and maybe in the universe: 6,400 forms of life in the category to which we belong—fewer, I'm guessing, than the number of different styles of dress shoes out there in the world.

In a minor way, I am part wine grape (percentage of shared DNA: 24) and part roundworm (percentage of shared DNA: 21 to 38). At the same time, though, I am at least four-fifths of a genetic match with a cheetah, a snow monkey, a blue whale, a bat (at least one of every five mammal species is some type of bat), a bat-eared fox, an ermine, a wild yak—and the last of the beautiful saola antelopes, discovered in 1992 in the mountains of Laos and Vietnam and now perhaps a few dozen survivors away from extinction; last of the little vaquita porpoises, whose numbers have fallen below twenty in the northern Gulf of California; last of the tool-making orangutans disappearing in Borneo and Sumatra. This is some of my greater self, disappearing out there; some of your greater self too.

. . .

As I paddled to correct for the drift of the outgoing tide and to keep an eye on the grizzly mothers and cubs, my memory returned to another rangy young bear met years earlier in a different section of the estuary. I was afoot with five other people on the shoreline then. We were checking one of the sites where the researcher Barrie Gilbert, a professor of animal behavior and

This rhinoceros dung beetle, a type of scarab, is just one of the about 400,000 beetle species known so far. By contrast, there are only about 6,400 living species of mammals.
PIOTR NASKRECKI/ MINDEN PICTURES

Now critically endangered, the saiga is native to the steppes of Eurasia. Its distinctively long, tubular nose is thought to help filter dust and warm frigid winter air during this antelope's long migrations.
TIM FLACH

wildlife management from Utah State University, had previously placed a scent lure and some sticky material he hoped would snag fur from curious bears. From the DNA in such hair samples, he could identify individual grizzlies and their degree of kinship with others here and piece together a detailed picture of the area's population makeup.

We spied the bear walking a good distance away. A few moments later, it paused and stared in our direction. (The popular notion that grizzlies have terrible eyesight is bogus.) Then the animal started moving again but on a new course. With binoculars, I took a closer look at the animal. And said to myself, *Oh boy. Here we go.* We had attracted the interest of a four- or five-year-old male, the grizzly equivalent of a teenager. I would have bet that he was going to make an indirect loop designed to end up near our little group. He did exactly that, wading through the tidal shallows at a faux-casual pace until he was on the same strand of shoreline where we stood. In grizzly social protocol, a direct stare can be a challenge, and Teen Grizz was taking care to look in every direction except directly at us—a good sign, but he kept strolling our way until he was within ten feet.

Then he turned sideways, as if to give us a view of his size, which was not huge but nevertheless impressive. He made a show of grazing the few sedges on the beach and of snuffling around the tidal rocks coated with algae and barnacles as though they offered the most exquisite seafood in the region. This adolescent wasn't acting as though he planned to add a person to his diet next. To me, what he was really doing was telling us: "I'm a grizzly bear feeding right here, practically in your face. How do you like it?" He probably wasn't quite sure of exactly how powerful he was, but his confidence had been growing along with his size, and so here he was, bold and curious, come to test things out—see who's who and what's what.

Using a calm tone, Gilbert told us, "Don't back away, or he could become a problem for anyone visiting here later. Stay close and let him know he can't intimidate us." We stayed put. It wasn't all that brave a choice. Several of us carried bear spray—a canister of heavy oil mixed with capsicum, the "hot" in hot chili peppers. When it contacts the eyes and nose, it feels like fire and can leave an aggressor breathless and disoriented. We had the cans out and aimed and stood ready to press the plunger if the young male pushed much closer. Stalemate. Teen Grizz took a couple more half-hearted bites of vegetation, side-eyeing us, lingered for a time that felt much longer than it probably was, and finally left—making a point of going very slowly, looking back toward us now and then. "Be ready," the researcher warned. "This is when some will suddenly turn and try a bluff charge to find out if you'll give way."

How many people have spent enough time negotiating at close range with grizzlies to be able to offer an observation like that? I've been charged a few times by these bears and charged as well by black rhinos, Indian one-horned rhinos, Asian elephants, African elephants, a lion, a grey reef shark, and probably some other animals I've forgotten about. I came out OK, but I don't remember keeping my cool in any of those situations. By contrast, Gilbert couldn't have been more outwardly calm. This was all the more impressive since, early in his career, he had lost part of his face, including an eye, during an attack by a grizz he surprised—and tried to run from—on a Yellowstone mountainside. Since recovering, he had spent decades studying these bears from Yellowstone to Katmai National Park on the Alaska

Peninsula, becoming steadily more expert at gauging their body language and serving as a strong voice for better management to protect them. I trusted the judgment of this remarkable man.

The charge to test us never came. Our confrontational young animal merely moved on and disappeared around a bend in the shoreline. Now, every motive and attitude I've ascribed to the bear in this encounter could be completely wrong. I don't know how a grizzly bear's mind works. But I felt sure all along about one thing: This animal had ambled over to where we were for the same reason we went there in the first place—to try to find out more about another kind of creature.

You can describe a grizzly bear with any terms you want: wilderness icon or unholy monster, mountain monarch or leftover barrier to civilization's progress. Those are labels for a character in the tales humans tell about themselves and their own desires. In real life, we and this master mammal are much more alike than not, genetically and physically—and kindred spirits insofar as both of us are curious about the world and live a fairly long time, learning all the while. Beyond the raw strength grizzlies possess, part of the power we sense in them is that intelligence we share. All those commonalities are the when-I-met-a-great-big-bear story that I think is worth spreading around.

NEXT SPREAD

Grizzlies can live for thirty-five years. This worn-looking female may have lost some of her facial fur by nosing into the rock rubble to get at plump army cutworm moths resting among the stones. Glacier National Park, Montana.
STEVEN GNAM

... we and this master mammal are much more alike than not ... kindred spirits insofar as both of us are curious about the world and live a fairly long time, learning all the while.

Ka-Boom

There always seem to be plenty of voices insisting that problems for the environment and wildlife are not anywhere near as dire as the eco-activists would have you believe. Others say the truth lies in between what the gloom-and-doom gang wants you to worry about and what the everything's-peachy pack wants you to ignore. So how does the situation for the species we share this planet with really look these days? Be honest.

I will. But I'm not going to try to convince anyone that this planet is changing as never before. During its roughly 4.5 billion-year history, Earth has been subjected to meteor strikes that beat the crap out of it; massive volcanic activity, some possibly caused by the bombardment from space; reversals of the magnetic poles; severe fluctuations in climate; and dramatic changes in the chemistry of the atmosphere and oceans caused by forces still unclear. Most paleontologists think the first living creatures arose almost 4 billion years ago. Since then, despite upheavals, the process of life producing new life was never broken as far as anyone can tell. But it did get very seriously bent.

Fossil evidence reveals five episodes when a major percentage of the organisms on the planet disappeared within a brief interval of geologic time. The communities of creatures that emerged after each upheaval were quite different, and for them to reach the levels of abundance and variety previously achieved took several million years—the equivalent of a couple hundred thousand human generations. Not that any humans were around at the time. The last big collapse took place 65 to 66 million years ago and marked the close of the dinosaurs' long reign. However, another global die-off is taking place right now. Not only are we humans here to witness this one, but we are also the cause of it.

Here's a two-minute history of what's been going on since *Homo sapiens* first appeared roughly 350,000 years back: 97 percent of those years came and went before humankind's total global population exceeded 1 million, perhaps sometime between 12,000 BCE and 10,000 BCE. We hit the 50 million mark around 1000 BCE, when Iron Age kingdoms were competing for power in India and David was the king of the Israelites. Then boom! By about 1800 CE, our numbers had increased 1,900 percent to our first billion.

The same century saw the onset of the Industrial Revolution. Ka-Boom!

After the mid-1800s, the human population growth pattern began to resemble that of bacteria on a good feed, doubling in number over ever-shorter periods. In just two and a half decades between the year I was born and the time I began working as a wildlife biologist, humanity added 1.3 billion more members. Since then, our numbers have more than doubled to nearly 8 billion—with more powerful new machinery and technology at our disposal. Go to Delhi, Mexico City, Beijing, or Los Angeles at rush hour, or to Canada's tar sands mining operations trans-

As the number of people was roughly doubling in the forty-two years between 1970 and 2012, the total population count of the planet's wild animals ... fell by more than half.

forming northern Alberta, and you can picture the consequences more easily. Every four or five days now, the planet has to provide room and sustenance for as many additional human beings as existed worldwide in 10,000 BC. More scholars have begun to refer to this modern period as a new phase of Earth's history, the Anthropocene (Human Epoch), in recognition of the fact that we are reshaping the world with the force of a geologic change.

It is argued that the quality of life for the majority of people is better today than it has been in the past. That appears to be true by some measures. We certainly like to believe that it is, but we have no sure way to judge how rewarding our ancestors found their place in the world to be compared with folks today. What we do know is that the rate at which natural resources are currently being depleted to support the swelling ranks of humanity is unsustainable, as is the buildup of harmful waste products in crowded locales and the spread of pollutants around the globe.

Here's the situation for other-than-humans: A major hallmark of the Anthropocene has been the switch from a steady increase in the diversity and abundance of life forms since the dinosaurs' demise to a pattern of relentless decline. The number of species extinctions continues to rise steeply upward in parallel with the human population growth chart. Judging from the fossil record, this present-day rate at which species are vanishing appears to be several hundred to several thousand times higher than the average going back hundreds of millions of years—long before the dinosaurs' demise.

As the number of people was roughly doubling in the forty-two years between 1970 and 2012, the total population count of the planet's wild animals (defined as the vertebrates—fish, amphibians, reptiles, birds, and mammals) fell by more than half. That statistic came from the Living Planet Report produced by the World Wildlife Fund, the Zoological Society of London, and other partner organizations. Their updated Living Planet Report released in 2020, based on counts of 20,811 populations of 4,392 vertebrate species sampled around the globe, was still more alarming: This new tally showed that by 2016, the decline in wild animal numbers since 1970 had already risen to nearly 70 percent. In other words, of every every ten wild animals that roamed Earth half a century ago, only three stand in their place today.

Close to 95 percent of the total biomass (living weight) of all the mammals on Earth's land surface now consists solely of humans and their livestock. Among surviving wild mammals, the most at risk are two types. The first tend to be small and restricted to a particular habitat or locale that can be all too easily obliterated. The second type are large-bodied species simply running out of places to fit into today's world alongside coming-right-up-on-eight-billion of us. A full 60 percent of the wild plant-eaters, or herbivores, weighing more than 220 pounds (100 kilograms) and 59 percent of the predators, or carnivores, weighing more than 33 pounds (15 kilograms) are currently considered threatened with extinction. About one-quarter of the 6,400 mammal species in existence today fall into the threatened category according to the leading global authority on the subject, the International Union for the Conservation of Nature. Among humankind's closest relatives, the primates, at least three-quarters of the species that exist are declining and at least one-third are imperiled.

The percentage of birds threatened with extinction stands at 14; for reptiles, 15 to 20; for amphibians, it's more than 40 percent. Although the vast oceans haven't been inventoried well enough to provide good estimates for fish, no one disputes that virtually all the main species targeted by commercial fisheries are drastically depleted. The global population of seabirds, which are dependent upon fish, has plummeted 70 percent since the 1950s. Because skates and rays favor shallow waters, making them easier to survey than open ocean swimmers, biologists know that 30 percent of these fish are imperiled.

Invertebrate animals are generally much smaller than vertebrates and less conspicuous, but they were so abundant that their numbers were seldom closely tracked. However, regular insect surveys did get carried out in a few parts of Europe and North America, and they reveal alarming declines of 75 percent or more over recent decades. Which may be one of the major factors behind the loss of nearly three of every ten birds in North

1970
2016

CHAPTER TWO

TOTAL LIVING WEIGHT OF LAND-DWELLING MAMMALS WORLDWIDE
Wildlife   Humans   Livestock

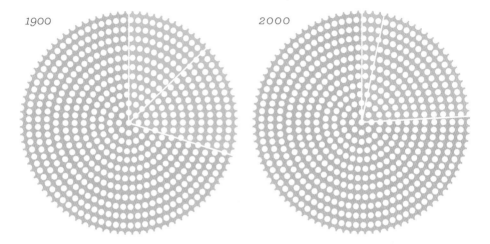

1900

2000

America during the past half-century, according to a 2019 paper in *Science* magazine by Cornell University researchers. A 2019 United Nations Global Environment Outlook report estimated the share of invertebrates at risk of extinction to be 25 percent for marine species, 34 percent for freshwater species, and 42 percent for the land-based species. These lower tiers of the animal-life pyramid support every level above them, including the ones occupied by humankind and the big animals we pay more attention to. And when the foundation of a pyramid is rapidly eroding away, it surely doesn't bode well for the top.

A recent mapping project by the Wildlife Conservation Society in coordination with NASA and Columbia University reveals that the current footprint of human activities covers more than four-fifths of the planet's ice-free land surface and

Amazonian deforestation in the state of Rondônia, western Brazil. Besides removing wildlife habitats wholesale, cutting and burning woodlands releases massive amounts of stored carbon, accelerating global warming.
MICHAEL NICHOLS

virtually every fertile acre suitable for growing crops. Four out of every five land-dwelling species of plants and animals live in forests. Over the past three centuries, people have stripped off 40 percent of Earth's woodland cover and altered about 82 percent of what remains. This 82 percent figure may be an underestimate, notably in stretches of the tropics where the vegetation still stands mostly intact but guns, pit traps, and miles of wire snares lacing the ground remove most of the fauna of any size.

The portions of tropical forests defined as true rainforests cloak a minor amount of the planet's land—about 7 percent. But together, they still harbor half of the world's species identified

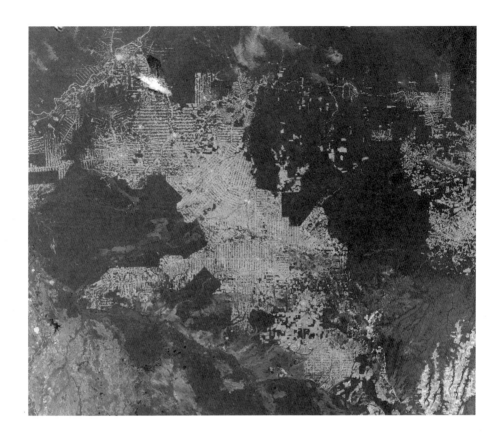

to date, including two-thirds of the species of flowering plants. Each day, an estimated 80,000 tropical rainforest acres are cut down and replaced by human habitats, and 80,000 more are altered by partial cutting, water diversion, pollution, and other human activities. That translates into a total of 91,000 square miles—roughly the combined area of the states of New Jersey, New York, Massachusetts, Vermont, and New Hampshire—lost or degraded per year. This is one reason that about 40 percent of the gymnosperms (the ancient group of plants bearing naked seeds, which includes cycads, ginkos, and conifers) are now on the imperiled list. For that matter, an extensive 2020 report

A satellite view reveals the extent of forest loss in Rondônia as of 2012. Roughly 82 percent of the world's remaining forests have now been altered by human activities. NASA

assembled by the Kew Royal Botanic Gardens in London, states that nearly 40 percent of all the known species of plants—and fungi as well—now appear at risk of extinction. Researchers are still a long way from discovering all the other life forms hidden within the tropics' tangled green recesses, but judging from sites where intensive sampling has been done, it looks as though the ongoing changes to these rainforests could be extinguishing 50,000 or more species of plants and animals annually.

Coral reefs, Earth's other great generators of biodiversity, occupy just a fraction of 1 percent of the oceans, yet are associated with almost a quarter of all known marine species. There are hundreds of different species of corals themselves. One in every three of those has been declared at risk of extinction. As for the reefs the corals build—the colorful mazes of nooks and crannies that support such dazzling congregations of other ocean life—most now fit one of the following categories: pushed out of balance by overfishing; sickened by pollution, ocean acidification, lower oxygen levels, and emerging diseases; bleached by unusually warm ocean temperatures; dying; or, as is the case for at least one-third of them around the world, recently deceased.

Particles and threads from the decomposition of plastic debris we dump into the seas are now present from the wind-patterned surface to the still, dark depths of marine trenches, and can be found in the bodies of virtually every category of animal in the marine food chain. Heavy metals and toxic carcinogens released as the plastics decay continue to accumulate in both the saltwater creatures and humans who consume seafood. Since plastics are manufactured from fossil fuels, this is equivalent to a worldwide oil spill that just keeps getting thicker. By 2050, the total amount of plastic in the oceans is expected to outweigh

Although coral reefs occupy less than 1 percent of the oceans, they are linked to the lives of 25 to 30 percent of all known marine species. TOMMY SCHULTZ

These corals are bleached and dead. If current rates of loss continue, 90 percent of Earth's coral reefs will be dead by this century's end due to rising sea temperatures. GARY BELL/ MINDEN PICTURES/ OCEANWIDE

CHAPTER TWO

the fish. That prediction, from the 2016 World Economic Forum, took into account a mid-century human population likely to surpass 10 billion and plans by the plastics industry for ramping up production to match the expected demand.

So ... where are we in the argument between environmentalists and those who dismiss them as alarmists? Well, things are getting pretty bad out there beyond the debate chambers. Honestly? It's close to terrifying. For an appalling share of Earth's life forms, the chances of survival through the rest of this century range from poor to zilch.

Manta rays sieve the water for zooplankton. How many microplastic particles and larger pieces of the trash here in Indonesia do you suppose this giant manta accidentally took in that day?
BROOKE LORI PYKE

. . .

The biosphere that supports us shows clear evidence of imbalance and fading vitality. Just as clearly, our century-old models of conserving nature are no longer suited to a planet whose human population has more than quadrupled since the early 1900s. An awful lot of standard conservation strategies were already irrelevant by the time I was taught them in college. Today, reliable authorities are pointing out that the Earth is on course to lose one-third to one-half of its known life forms by the end of the century, if not sooner. This can't be dismissed as the world having a few bad decades. On the geological time scale measured in centuries and millennia, this is your living planet suffering a stroke.

None of that is breaking news. People have been raising alarms about the Sixth Great Extinction for years. Yet the warnings have had little measurable effect. The slide toward large-scale extinctions within a human lifetime is accelerating. There are a number of reasons for this. But there aren't any good reasons to hastily discard the company and promise of so many fellow creatures. Not when we have so much yet to learn about the roles those other Earthlings play within ecosystems that we, too, depend upon. Not when we're just beginning to appreciate all the mechanisms encoded in their genes for staying healthy,

... nobody is really to blame for the present state of affairs. People are merely continuing to strive for more space and resources. It's what species do.

making unique materials, sensing the environment, communicating in ways we never considered—all the different skills those life forms embody for existing under various conditions, all the miraculous blueprints we might want or need to borrow one day.

While it's not surprising that our desire is to save the species that seem the most interesting or useful to us, this is not the best strategy for conserving the planet's biological diversity—its full array of life forms and all the processes and interactions associated with them. DNA contains chemically coded instructions for survival accumulated over billions of years, with every new generation adding refinements and innovations. Collectively, the millions of species in existence represent the largest and most elaborate store of information on Earth. What are we doing with this treasure? We're pursuing activities on track to extinguish as many as 50 percent of the known species by the century's end. It's like permanently deleting half the database files on the world's computers or (to put it in old-school terms) ripping out half the pages of the only edition of the *Book of Life*.

Referring to the present crisis as the Sixth Great Extinction period in Earth's long history is neither hype nor a full-on panic attack. Nor is it the outgrowth of an ideology or pressures from special interest groups. It is an honest assessment based on well-documented trends. The interest group that stands to benefit most from actions to reverse those trends is everyone (humans and all others) in the world.

Despite plenty of finger-pointing and name-calling, nobody is really to blame for the present state of affairs. People are merely continuing to strive for more space and resources. It's what species do. Our species is so skilled at displacing others that we have succeeded massively—even to the extent of altering the chemistry of the oceans and atmosphere, the appearance of entire landscapes, and the living contents of ecosystems. Nothing about that implies some flaw in human nature. What happened is that we evolved and adapted, just as every creature does, except we did not do it entirely through genes—the information coded in our DNA. We also did it through memes—the information coded in language and transmitted from one generation to the next through learning.

Other intelligent species also pass along learned information to offspring using their own vocalizations and body language. But no other creature does memes plus tools plus complex improvisation like modern *Homo sapiens*. The combination made us the all-time world champions in the contest for survival among large mammals, monopolizing (together with our livestock) more and more of the globe's available space. We now qualify not only as the foremost threat to all kinds of other Earthly life but also as the biggest obstacle to a secure tomorrow for ourselves.

· · ·

I'm more than ready to stop piling on depressing numbers and disaster scenarios in these pages. You're probably more than ready to stop reading them. Mind you, I'm not promising to quit cold. But since this is a book about a new understanding of nature and putting the insights to work in positive ways, I want to be sure to emphasize that the predicted genocide-scale losses of fellow creatures and the collapse of natural systems are just that: predictions. They are logical projections based on current trends, but they are not foreordained events. No outcome is inevitable as long as human behavior and inventiveness are part of the equation.

"Do unto ecosystems as you would have them do unto you." This new golden rule I suggest isn't meant to be taken as a high-minded moral obligation. At this stage of the Anthropocene, it's more like a practical survival strategy. We're talking about life insurance policies here.

A couple of centuries went by before it was no longer a punishable heresy to agree with Nicolaus Copernicus's conclusion in the first half of the sixteenth century that the Earth revolves around the Sun instead of sitting at the center of the universe. After Charles Darwin announced in his 1859 book *On the Origin of Species* and later in *The Descent of Man* that organisms don't stay exactly the same forever—that they evolve through natural selection and that we ourselves arose from earlier primates—it took more than half a century for a majority of the educated public to start getting comfortable with these discoveries. And they still have their share of deniers. Humanity and Earth's other inhabitants no longer have that kind of time to wait around for recent scientific revelations to replace outdated notions about nature.

The evidence calls for a thorough reset of our relationship with the rest of the living world. Such a realignment becomes crucial as mounting environmental crises overwhelm the natural world. But it's not clear how we'll find the will to move quickly enough to meet the challenge until we move beyond the idea of ourselves as special beings separate from nature. We have never been, and are not now, creatures apart from all the others. Humans, too, are naturals. If anything, science is telling us that we are more deeply embedded within the natural world in more ways than most people ever imagined.

NEXT SPREAD

A human infant reacts to being examined with a stethoscope during a checkup at a hospital. KRASULA/ SHUTTERSTOCK

Another infant belonging to a very similar species (percent of genes shared between lowland gorilla and human: 96) reacts the same way at the Melbourne Zoo in Victoria, Australia. DAVID CAIRD/ NEWS LTD./NEWSPIX

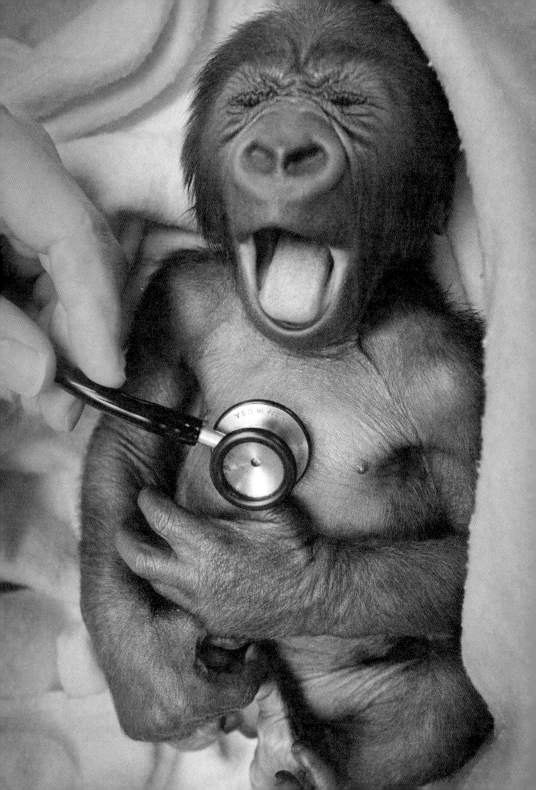

The Living Planet Quick Reference Guide

Scientists long depicted the world's variety of organisms in the form of a tree of life with what were thought of as primitive forms at the base and a spreading canopy of advanced and more evolved forms toward the crown. Those terms were misleading insofar as many of the creatures placed toward the bottom were not so much simple as merely small. These days, biologists recognize three distinct domains of life, each with its own branches fanning out in different directions and its own share of recently evolved and comparably advanced species.

Two of the domains consist of single-celled organisms called prokaryotes. Like all living things, they have DNA in the form of chromosomes, but this genetic material is not enclosed within a membrane to form a nucleus. Bacteria make up one of the prokaryote domains. The second is the archaea. Because many of its members look like bacteria, they were lumped together with them until the 1970s, when modern molecular studies uncovered fundamental genetic differences between these two groups of organisms. All of Earth's other life forms (as well as animals and

prokaryote
proh-kar-ee-oht

archaea
ahr-kee-uh

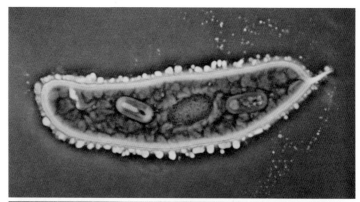

Euglena oxyuris is a single-celled freshwater life form with qualities of both a plant (with green chloroplasts to carry out photosynthesis) and an animal (with an eyespot and a whip-like "tail" for swimming).
BIOPHOTO ASSOCIATES/ SCIENCE SOURCE

Earth's oceans formed around 4.4 billion years ago. The first life may have developed in waters near volcanic sources of heat and minerals like this deep sea hydrothermal vent near the Galápagos Islands.
THE INSTITUTE OF GEOLOGICAL & NUCLEAR SCIENCES/ NOAA-OE/SCIENCE SOURCE

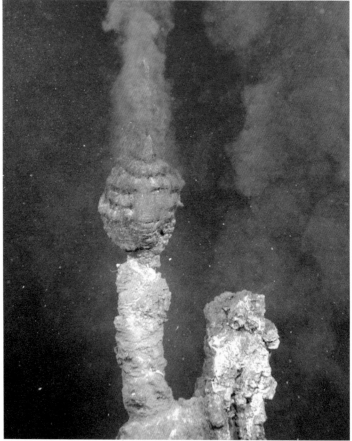

plants) are included in the third domain, the eukarya (or eukaryotes), distinguished by the membrane-bounded nucleus containing the chromosomes within each of their cells. Eukaryotes
probably arose from the archaea, for these two domains turn out
to be more similar to one another genetically than either one is
to the bacteria.

eukarya
yoo-keh-ree-ah

eukaryote
yoo-kar-ree-oht

Biologists divide the eukarya into four main categories. The
first is protists (sometimes called protozoans), a sort of catch-
all basket for single-celled organisms from a broad spectrum of
different groups such as amoebas, ciliates, and diatoms. Fungi,
from unicellular yeasts to subterranean mats the size of small
towns, make up the second division. The other divisions are the
two that every child learns at an early age: plants and animals.

protist
proh-tist

protozoan
proh-tuh-zoh-uhn

Not all eukaryotes fit readily into one of these categories.
For example, the thousand or more species of *euglenoids* are
single-celled critters with a long thrashing whip or two on one
end and a red eyespot. Quite a few are active predators and were
originally labeled animals. But most also have bodies stuffed with
green chloroplasts carrying on photosynthesis, leading other nat-
uralists to consider them plants. Then there is the puzzle of what
slime molds actually are. They reside in moist woodland settings
as tiny, independent amoeba-like cells that you'd never notice—
until they suddenly start to gather in response to some environmental cue and merge into a mass that looks like a spilled scoop
of jelly. Then it/they ooze-crawl over the forest floor for some distance before sending up a stalk with spores to reproduce.

euglenoids
yoo-gle-noydz

Past scientists declared slime molds atypical fungi or even
uncanny versions of an animal. Like the euglenoids and a good
many other outliers, slime molds ended up being squeezed
into the protist division. But such organisms still stand out as

reminders that nature isn't nearly as concerned with categories as the people who study it tend to be. That's life; it invents
new rules and possibilities as it goes along. An assortment of
archaea and bacteria emphasize this by blowing off a lot of the
basic rules that science used to assume all of Earth's beings were
bound by. Termed extremophiles, these prokaryotes flourish not
only in the boiling waters of hot springs on land and hydrothermal vents in the oceans' depths but also in cold submarine brine
seeps, on sunbaked desert salt pans, underneath ice caps, and
even in waters laden with acids or toxins draining from industrial sites. More dwell in subterranean aquifers miles deep within
the planet's crust. Others colonize the tiniest pores and cracks in
layers of otherwise solid stone, obtaining the energy they need
to survive by using enzymes to break the chemical bonds of mineral compounds.

A common freshwater colonial algae with thousands of cells, Volvox *takes the form of spheres within spheres. The small dark green globes are the newest daughter colonies.* FRANK FOX/SCIENCE PHOTO LIBRARY

If you picture the early days of Earth when it was a sphere
of hot rock and corrosive liquids, erupting with volcanoes in
an atmosphere of methane and sulfurous gases, you can understand why many scientists think extremophiles represent the
original life forms. They may also be representative of the kind
of extraterrestrials we're most likely to meet if we ever do find
life on a nearby planet.

One way or another, archaea, bacteria, protists, single-celled
versions of fungi, and algae—in short, the microbes—dominate
the biosphere in terms of total numbers and the numbers of species. They are everywhere in both freshwater and saltwater, in
the land and the air, on the surfaces of plants and animals, and
within their bodies. Bacteria are the most abundant and varied
group of all. They generally reproduce by simply splitting. Some
can grow and replicate themselves this way every four minutes.

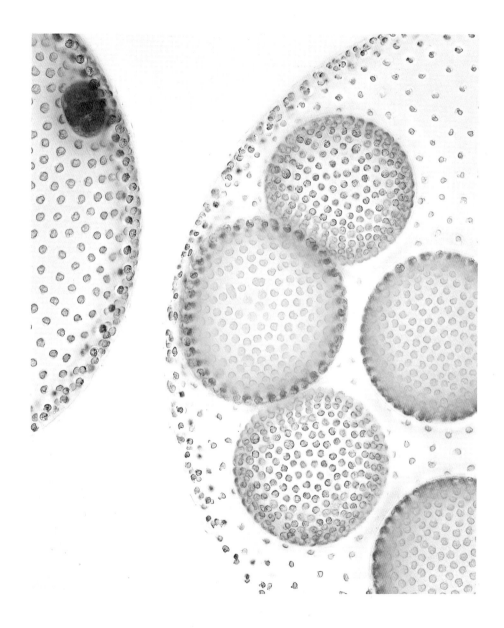

More typical species take about twenty minutes to accomplish that. Even at this slower rate, one cell could still generate a population covering the Earth six feet deep within twenty-four hours if none of the bacteria died. That's especially impressive since a hundred million bacteria piled together would only take up as much space as eight drops of water.

Subjected to harsh conditions, many bacteria respond by forming spores with a protective coating and going dormant. Scientists have revived some found in ice layers or dried debris thousands of years old. One laboratory even reactivated bacteria locked in salt crystals formed around 250 million years ago. Yet

Cyanobacteria like this ocean species, Prochlorococcus marinus, *played a major role in oxygenating the planet's early atmosphere and remain the most abundant photosynthetic organisms on Earth today.* LUKE THOMPSON, CHISHOLM LAB/ NIKKI WATSON, MIT

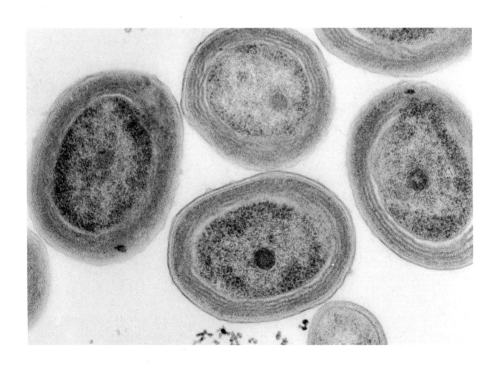

CHAPTER THREE

the typical life span of most bacteria is measured in mere hours. Just as every waste product a bacterium or other microbe expels is another microbe's banquet, so is every microbe's corpse. All this round-the-clock multiplying, dining, digesting, dying, and decomposing supports larger life forms all the way up the food chain by enriching soils, waters, and the very air itself.

A cyanobacterium called *Prochlorococcus*, superabundant in seawater and capable of photosynthesis, is believed to produce at least one-fifth of the oxygen in the atmosphere. Diatoms and other micro-algae raise that percentage to about one-half. Countless microbes on the surfaces of water, the ground, and the leaves of plants get aerosolized—swept up by winds and carried high into the sky. There, they attract water molecules, causing droplets to form. This is how living creatures seed rainclouds and influence weather around the globe, making microbes important players in the constant recycling of water between Earth's surface and its atmosphere.

cyanobacterium
sai-an-noh-bak-teer-ee-uhm

Prochlorococcus
Proh-klorih-caah-kiss

To those folks conditioned to thinking of microbes as enemies, all I can say is: Sorry, but together with every other eukaryote, we evolved from prokaryotes and live in a broth of them, and when we die they will decompose us and use the nutrients to compose more of themselves. This is pretty much the planet of the microbes and will remain so no matter how loudly we big creatures stomp around claiming dominion.

Now, if you were to take the beyond-astronomical number of microbes on Earth and multiply it by a hundred or even a thousand, the result might still be an underestimate for the total number of viruses in the biosphere. In case you're wondering why I didn't mention them until now, it's because biologists still haven't decided whether or not viruses meet the standard of being alive.

A virus is not quite the same as an organism. It is a quasi-being—a particle, a packet of molecules embodying genetic information (DNA or RNA or both) wrapped in a protein coat. Viruses can't replicate themselves without invading a living cell and borrowing—or commandeering—the machinery of that cell's chromosomes. During this process, the viruses sometimes pick up bits of genetic code from the cells they attack. The viruses' descendants may then transfer those pieces directly into the chromosomes of the next hosts they invade. Since viral bodies interact with species along most every strand in the web of life, they play a sort of wild card role in introducing novel traits to organisms at all levels from bacteria to vertebrates. Researchers are struggling to understand how strong and widespread this viral influence might be on the overall course of evolution—previously believed to depend mainly upon chance mutations. So far, the evidence points toward viruses playing a broader role than anyone had previously considered in both the emergence of new life forms and the balance of ecosystems.

By one estimate, 100,000 pieces of a human's DNA—around 8 percent of our genome—is viral material retained from infections in our ancestors dating back millions of years. Molecular biologists used to dismiss such sequences as "junk" DNA. They are now taking a hard second look after discovering that, for instance, a gene essential to the function of the human placenta is a repurposed sequence from a virus.

· · ·

Here, then, is your living planet, absolutely brimming with invisible dramas, the majority of them involving organisms only a few specialists even know the names of. When the rest of us picture nature, we're far more likely to have in mind a bird singing from a flowering bush or a tiger stalking through the shadows on a jungle floor. We can't help it; these are the dimensions our species is attuned to. Because most of Earth's species are too small for humans to see, we have no real sense of them going about their lives or of their populations conducting flows of energy and nutrients through ecosystems. We're not conscious of the genes we share with that songbird or that tiger or the genes we have in common with near-infinite numbers of microbes. Most people have no idea that their DNA incorporates pieces introduced by viruses ancient and new.

I happen to be writing portions of this book while sequestered at home during the COVID-19 pandemic of 2020. Worldwide, the disease is claiming several thousand human lives daily and disrupting the lives of billions week after week, leaving unemployment, hunger, fear, and grieving in its wake. Since the outbreak began, I've felt odd working to show that humankind is inseparable from nature while a wild coronavirus is taking advantage of exactly that fact in a harrowing way. Still, I believe it is the right time for a thorough look at our relationship with nature, because so many of the bonds that tie us to it are the ones that keep us alive and healthy.

Heads up: Every time you take a breath, you're inhaling viruses by the thousands. About 800 million drift down from the sky onto every square yard of ground on the globe every day. That isn't scary. These are just statements of fact—and proof that very, very few of the viruses humans come into contact with ever do anything to us. As for the rare ones that can cause problems, you have a remarkable immune system on call for help in fending them off. Similarly, only a very tiny percentage of the untold

CHAPTER THREE

millions of species of bacteria out there are known to cause disease in humans, and our immune system typically keeps most of those in check.

Look, I worry about COVID-19 as much as anybody else. I worry, too, about the environmental problems we face. A majority of them are predictable consequences of human overpopulation. These include extreme concentrations of humans and their habitations, serious overcrowding of livestock, exploitation of wild animal populations in remote areas for distant food markets—among them the traditional live, or "wet," markets in urban centers of Asia—and levels of pollution and stress that weaken immune systems. Such conditions raise the chances of a disease spilling over from animals to people and from one person to the next. Combined with two larger-scale effects linked to human overpopulation—climate change and the destabilizing of ecosystems—these factors make future outbreaks inevitable.

One way or another, the current pandemic will eventually wind down. The environmental issues won't. They will keep mounting until we respond to them with the same intense focus and push for a universal cure that societies have mustered in the face of COVID-19.

More than one in five mammal species is a bat. They are essential ecosystem pollinators and insect-eaters, but some, like these Egyptian fruit bats in a Uganda forest cave, host viruses lethal to humans. JOEL SARTORE

NEXT SPREAD

Sometimes described as algae that live in glass houses, diatoms are photosynthetic protists that construct shells of pure silica. This marine species grows in clusters on seaweeds. WIM VAN EGMOND

The State of Our Union

There is so much nature in human nature that I can't see where any more could fit in. To begin with, the number of distinctly human cells in each human being, variously estimated at 20 to 40 trillion, is equaled or exceeded by the number of microbe cells.

Close to a thousand different species inhabit your mouth. Several thousand species dwell within your digestive tract. Hundreds of species or more reside almost everywhere else. They coat your skin, line your pores, cling to your hairs, and especially abound in all the damp spots. Relax, I'm not judging; the same conditions apply to all of us, recently bathed or not.

Granted, a great many of the microscopic life forms we pack around are merely opportunists taking advantage of the nutrients to be found in and on a body as immense relative to their size as the planet is to a person. Although some of our occupants are the kind that can make us sick under certain conditions, most are either harmless, assist us with bodily functions, or actively protect us against disease-causing germs and toxins. Many help us resist other types of afflictions as well. To choose a recently discovered example, the common and harmless skin bacterium *Staphylococcus epidermidis* produces a molecule that may arrest the growth of cancer cells triggered by overexposure to the sun's ultraviolet rays.

A prime share of our gut microbes break down organic materials that we either can't digest or don't digest very efficiently. Some manufacture vitamins and other nutrients that we are either poor at making or unable to make and rarely get enough of from the foods we eat. As much as 80 percent of our immune system is situated in our gut, and its effectiveness

Staphylococcus epidermidis
Staf-uh-luh-caah-kiss ep-id-der-my-dis

A magnified and color-enhanced look at the kind of bacterial menagerie that thrives among the mucous membranes of your mouth.
MARTIN OEGGERLI, MICRONAUT

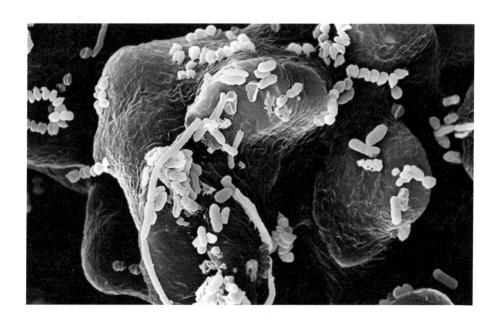

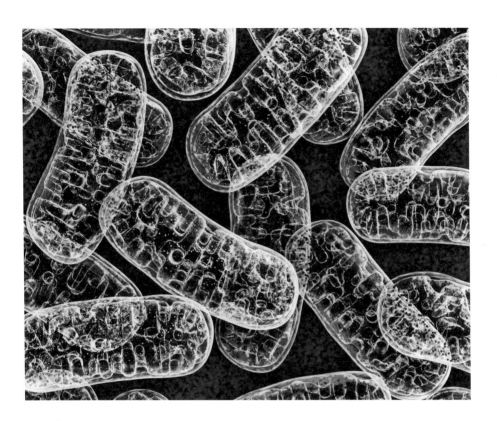

Mitochondria close-up. These are the ancient line of bacteria that now live as specialized organelles inside the cells of nearly every protist and multicellular organism, manufacturing the chemical energy that powers cell activity.
WIROMAN/ISTOCK

appears linked to the balance of species in the microbiome there. And several kinds of common gut bacteria have been found to manufacture hormones and neurotransmitters identical to those produced by human cells and capable of influencing our moods and activities. More researchers are beginning to view our gut microbiome as something like a big, complicated, and still mostly mysterious gland.

A flurry of research now underway is aimed at discovering how the microbes we host may be influencing not only our general health but also our momentary cravings, moods, and—ultimately—our thoughts. The implications are obviously enormous. Who's in charge of you? New findings may revolutionize medical treatments and personal wellness regimes, but the investigations are still in the preliminary stages. Meanwhile, think about adding more fiber from fruits and vegetables to your diet; it increases the variety of microbial allies in your gut and encourages their growth and metabolic activity.

Every person has about 22,000 (some put the estimate closer to 25,000) genes, the inherited set of chemically coded instructions that build and maintain a *Homo sapiens*. The spectrum of microbial beings we host possess at least 8 million genes among them, and I've seen estimates as high as 45 million. From this perspective, the full genome each of us carries around is a mosaic of human and microbe DNA, with the human part making up a very minor portion of the whole.

Bill Bryson calculates in his book *The Body: A Guide for Occupants* that if you were to uncoil all the DNA packed into your trillions of human cells and lay it end to end to form a single strand, it would extend for 10 billion miles from wherever you are to a point past Pluto. Though the DNA in each cell is the same, this is a stunning way to envision the total amount that a fully grown human being contains. And in reality, your greater self operates with even more. So, try mentally adding to that strand all the DNA from the microbes you host and picture a filament reaching still farther beyond this solar system toward the distant stars.

In addition to the number of life forms that make their homes alongside the cells of our bodies, don't forget the microbes dwelling *within* those cells as part of their make-up. Our cells can't function normally without the organelles, or internal pieces, labeled mitochondria, for they carry out the energy-generating chemical reactions that are the basis of our metabolism. Just a

Taken together, the invisible multitudes on and in us redefine every person as a kind of compound creature, an organism that is in reality a combination of organisms interwoven in more ways than we have yet found words to acknowledge.

few decades ago, scientists finally figured out that these organelles are actually modified ancient bacteria. As such, they add tens of trillions more microorganisms to the "you" that your mind conceives of as a singular being. Taken together, the invisible multitudes on and in us redefine every person as a kind of compound creature, an organism that is in reality a combination of organisms interwoven in more ways than we have yet found words to acknowledge.

This is not to say each person isn't an individual with a unique physical appearance, temperament, set of experiences, and so on. Combined with the intense level of self-awareness humans possess, this distinctive identity is very real to us and plays a preeminent role in both our relationships with other people and our position in society. Yet the importance we place upon our individuality becomes something of an obstacle to recognizing everything else that defines us. The microbes we are endowed with and the genes we have in common with other life forms are key dimensions of the human being.

Humankind's defining characteristics embody nature in other ways as well. Our nervous system, reflexes, senses, physical abilities, emotions, aspects of our social behavior and cultures, and even our thought patterns and decision-making abilities—many of the qualities we sum up as human nature— developed under the influences of predators, competitors, and the species we relied upon for food. Through the ages, whole communities of wild creatures large and small played parts in shaping who we are and what we do. They live on in modern people, just as part of what makes us human exists in the creatures around us today in the genes, tissues, metabolic pathways, and behaviors we have in common. This is what makes us more than just human. This is what I mean when I refer to our greater selves.

. . .

I relate to the world in an "I, me, mine" frame of mind but in reality, I function as an "us." Everybody does. Sharing genes with all other life forms; hosting prodigious numbers of microbes in and on our bodies; and having been shaped in form, function, and thought by interactions with other species turn out to be just three of the hallmarks that confirm us as more than human. The concept of our greater selves covers a still broader range. Case in point: I was a single-celled creature myself years ago. I'm not talking abstractly about being descended from some ancient archaean or other microbe. I'm describing my own physical start to life. It took place in my mother's womb as a just-fertilized egg—one cell measuring 0.004 inches in diameter. There are algae, protozoans, and even a few kinds of bacteria that were bigger than me. But, hey, I had plans.

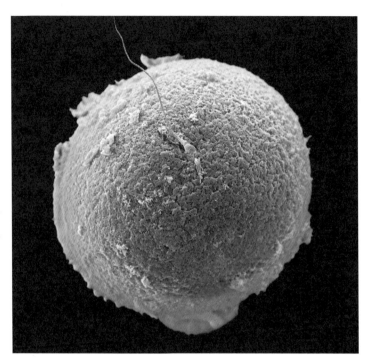

Two microorganisms, or microbes, viewed with a scanning electron microscope and artificially colored for clarity. They are a human egg and sperm, and their meeting is the prelude to fertilization.
EYE OF SCIENCE/ SCIENCE SOURCE

Within a day, I subdivided into a blob of cells that wasn't much larger overall, but those new cells grew and kept on dividing. By day four, they began to differentiate from one another and organize in patterns that would soon enough turn me into a little, comma-shaped thing with a vaguely defined head. I did not, as some once believed, go on to retrace the stages of vertebrate evolution by becoming fishlike, then amphibian-like, etc., as I developed. But I did share internal similarities with those groups as well as some physical resemblances at various stages; hardly surprising, since we had a majority of our genes in common.

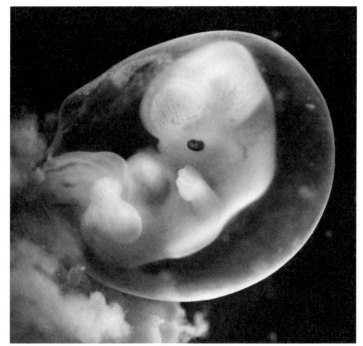

Just seven weeks after the single-celled human sperm and egg combine their chromosomes, natural genetic engineering has already produced a recognizable head, eyes, and budding limbs. LENNART NILSSON/SCIENCE PHOTO LIBRARY

Soon enough, I was growing into a miniature mammal, bathed in my mother's liquids while growing directly from her body via a fleshy connection funneling her blood and nutrients my way. Genes switched the myriad of me-building processes on and off in the right programmed sequence to add more details while I swelled all the way to eight pounds. I'd already been colonized by some microbes from my mother's blood and amniotic fluids, and during passage through the birth canal, I gained a whopping fresh batch of microbes even before I finally slid out into the world at large and breathed air for the first time.

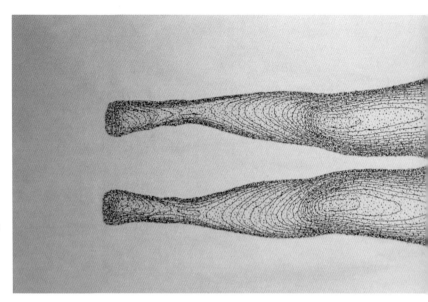

Not to brag, but that was one sensational effort by those 22,000 to 25,000 different genes within the fertilized egg that had expanded into a newborn me—one miraculous orchestration of more than 3 billion nucleotide base pairs, the organic chemical compounds making up my DNA. Yet everything about this inconceivably complex manufacturing of a human being was just business as usual for nature, guided by assembly instructions embedded in self-replicating molecules with portions of their coding relatively new and other portions that were old before life came out of the sea onto land. They speak eloquently of my more-than-human condition. The results of some 4 billion years of experimentation by nature were at work assembling me from the instant of conception.

. . .

But let's talk about you for a while. Suppose you decide to walk from your workplace to a deli for lunch and end up taking a

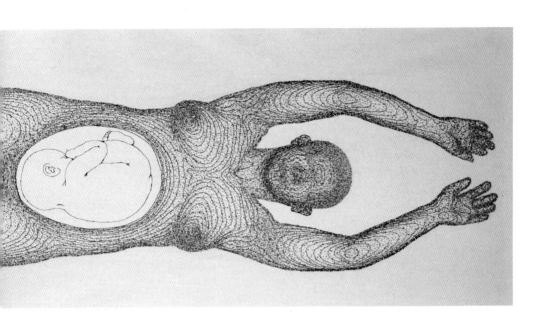

shortcut through a park. Something marvelous is about to happen. As you pass through the entrance, maybe your mind is on a news item you read earlier or something a coworker said, and you aren't thinking about nature in the least. Doesn't matter. Nature quickly starts to improve your overall health and prospects for longevity anyway.

You are being nurtured.

Your heart rate slows and becomes steadier. Your blood pressure decreases. Your body's level of relaxation increases; a specialist could tell how much by measuring the drop in your levels of cortisol and adrenaline, two key hormones symptomatic of stress. Meanwhile, your immune system gets a boost. Our imaginary specialist keeping you company (with an imaginary backpack full of lab equipment) could measure that too, first by the ramp-up in activity of your natural killer (NK) cells, which attack disease-causing viruses, harmful bacteria, and tumors; and, second, by the downtrend of cytokines, proteins associated with chronic inflammation that can lead to cardiovascular disease, diabetes, and depression, among other maladies.

As long as we've got someone along analyzing your biochemistry, let's check on your DHEA (dehydroepiandrosterone). This is a steroid hormone produced by the adrenal gland, your gonads, and your brain. It's more prevalent now that you're out among natural features, giving you better protection against heart problems, obesity, and diabetes. You'll likely register an increase in the protein hormone adiponectin as well. It reduces high blood glucose levels that can lead to obesity and type 2 diabetes, and it counters the plaque build-up in arteries that causes atherosclerosis.

dehydroepiandrosterone
dee-hai-droh-eh-pee-an-draa-str-own

Finally, the odds are high that your level of alertness is changing from one of intense or fixed concentration to a more general awareness. Described as attention restoration, an equally important feature of becoming more relaxed, this shift makes you less susceptible to mental fatigue and to the accidents that can result from that state. It tends to improve your impulse control as well, which can reduce the likelihood of indulging in risky health behaviors such as excessive drinking, drug use, smoking, and overeating. You'll probably sleep better tonight, too. Your only quality at risk of deteriorating is your reputation as a party animal.

If you went into the park and just sat on a bench rather than moving around and gaining the benefits of exercise, the physiological and psychological changes just described would still occur to some degree. They could happen if you bypassed the park completely and merely stopped to take in the sight of a curbside garden. Or if you did no more than look at images of trees, flowers, or natural landscapes on a screen inside a room. Or closed your eyes and inhaled essential oils from certain evergreen trees, other types of plants, or just their blossoms. Or went from an environment with noises such as traffic and machinery to some quieter setting. The more natural the source of any sounds you do hear in that new spot, the more beneficial your body's responses are likely to be.

In a green space, even a small urban park with trees, you're breathing better air too. Compared to its surroundings, the site has less carbon dioxide, since some has been absorbed by the leaves and the surprising abundance of microscopic algae that thrive in ponds and puddles but also on the soil surface. And you'll have a bit more oxygen to inhale, courtesy of the photosynthesis going on in the plants around you. Larger green spaces such as swaths of forest and mountainsides, especially where running water is present, also generate higher concentrations of negative ions. They help purify the air by causing particulates such as dust or industrial pollutants to clump together and fall to the ground. There is some additional evidence that negative ions influence chemical pathways in the body that relieve stress and depression.

Something else you might be drawing into your lungs from a green space are those essential oils from plants, which include volatile organic compounds called phytoncides. Formulated mainly to repel certain microbes and insects that attack vegetation, phytoncides have the effect in humans of lowering blood pressure and boosting immune system functions, primarily by stimulating the activity of natural killer cells. Some studies found phytoncides significantly increased subjects' energy levels and later improved their sleep.

phytoncides
fy-ton-sides

Lastly, you are being exposed to a natural diversity of microbes that might enrich the balance of your own skin and gut microbiomes. The mechanisms for that are not well defined, but experiments have shown that one particular soil mini-creature, *Mycobacterium vaccae*, appears to bolster the immune system, relieve anxiety, and improve learning in mice. It is now being investigated for possible use in human immunotherapy to treat asthma, psoriasis, cancer, and other ailments.

My intention isn't to make any of these effects sound instant, spectacularly effective, or even widely accepted as proven beyond any doubt. Many medical professionals, especially in Western countries, remain skeptical of the findings. Although the physiological changes I outlined have been documented in volunteers tested before and after exposure to natural stimuli—usually a green setting outdoors—there are a myriad of variables in play in different locations. Results differ from study to study, making them tricky to interpret. They change with the size and composition of the green space, the length of time subjects remained there, and whether they visited the setting once or repeatedly. Effects can also differ with the individual personalities of the subjects. In certain experiments, the conclusions may have been skewed by the benefits that people who are not normally very physically active gained just from the exercise of walking. In others tests, the positive changes recorded could simply reflect the power of positive thinking—the placebo effect—in subjects.

That said, the data on the whole remain convincing. The results were especially striking when the subjects' responses to a green space were compared with their responses to an urban street setting. The human heartbeat and blood chemistry don't lie. Exposure to nature—even for a relatively brief period, and even indirectly as with viewing natural objects on a screen—tends to lower stress and boost the immune system.

Mycobacterium vaccae
My-koh-bak-tee-ree-uhm vac-key

CHAPTER FOUR

The causes behind these outcomes are closely tied to the workings of the autonomic nervous system. This is the system that runs the involuntary functions of the body, from your breathing and the beating of your heart to the passing of food through your digestive tract. The human autonomic nervous system has two main divisions: the sympathetic system, usually described as controlling the muscles and glands that prepare the body for fight-or-flight reactions, and the parasympathetic system that promotes a restorative state—good old rest and relaxation.

What's going on is that many modern activities—like driving in heavy traffic; working for hours at a computer; or just contending with the crowds of strangers, clutter, noises, and other distractions of urban life—stimulate the sympathetic system and activate the body's fight-or-flight preparations. That overwhelms the parasympathetic system, reducing the ability of your body and mind to rest and relax. The opposite occurs in a tranquil natural landscape; the sympathetic system effects diminish, and the parasympathetic system effects come to the fore. As a result, feelings of stress are reduced along with muscle tension. Intense mental concentration gives way to a more reflective awareness, nicely described in one scientific paper as a "somewhat effortless, 'soft fascination.'" Sensations of calm and ease take over, whether you're conscious of them or not. Take them; they're free, a gift from the green world and your ancestors.

NEXT SPREAD

A Licuala fan palm canopy in the rainforest of Daintree National Park on the coast of northeastern Australia. KONRAD WOTHE/MINDEN PICTURES

Fluorescent corals, Favia, on the Great Barrier Reef of Australia resemble miniature palm forests. JURGEN FREUND/MINDEN PICTURES

Health Coverage for Primates

From a comfortable rainforest perch in a remote part of the Democratic Republic of the Congo, a young male chimpanzee strips bark for a meal.
IAN NICHOLS

Cultures around the world have long recognized natural settings as a balm for the soul. The notable exceptions were periods when countries in Europe, and later the United States, branded wild lands as unpredictable, dangerous, even demonic places. The rhetoric of the day equated natural with savage, an affront to order and progress, reinforcing the view that it was humankind's duty to eradicate or at least "civilize"—gain control over—what was not tamed. And yet the same Western societies also went through periods when nature was heavily romanticized as a source of unspoiled beauty, solitude, and renewal.

Early nineteenth-century transcendentalists such as Margaret Fuller, Henry David Thoreau, and Ralph Waldo Emerson espoused direct immersion in nature, rather than the study of formal doctrines, as a path to spiritual liberation. Their philosophy underpinned America's first efforts to establish nature

CHAPTER FIVE

reserves and still influences wildland conservation thinking in this country. Partially as a counterweight to the developing Industrial Revolution, city fathers and philanthropists began to push for the creation of urban parks, citing their benefits to public health. Hospitals and rest homes made a point of constructing grassy courtyards and gardens where possible. It's no accident that quite a few people tend vegetable gardens for more than the food they yield, just as many, consciously or unconsciously, keep houseplants for more than their virtues as décor.

An ancient Buddhist cemetery in Koyasan, Japan. What better setting to counter the sting of death than a quiet green space in the embrace of trees whose life spans are measured in centuries? LA CHOUETTE/ GETTY IMAGES/ ISTOCKPHOTO

Japan has been a leading source of recent research into the healing powers of contact with nature, perhaps not surprising in a nation with a tradition of forest-bathing. The practice has nothing to do with getting wet. *Shinrin-yoku*, as it is called, implies "absorbing the forest atmosphere through all our senses," taking in leaf patterns, colors, scents, the antiquity and grandeur of the trees, the sighs of breezes in their branches, the verdant tang of the air. In Japan and South Korea, immersion in a woodland setting to refresh the spirit and stimulate healing is considered therapeutic enough that guided forest-bathing sessions are covered by health insurance plans. In the West, more physicians are beginning to give their patients prescriptions to spend time outdoors.

During a recent trek along an old pilgrimage trail through the mountains of southern Japan, I passed into a commercial forest of Japanese cedars where the young trees had been felled to favor growth of the older ones. But instead of hauling away the downed trees, which were too small to be marketable, the loggers had cut the trunks into sections and arranged several pieces at a time side by side on the ground amid ferns and low-growing herbs. Softly weathered and coated with patchworks of lichens and mosses, the bed-size platforms looked like perfect places for a rest. And indeed, they were meant for that. A small sign invited foot-weary wayfarers to stretch out on the logs and forest bathe.

I shed my pack and lay on my back—thank you—to watch the feathery dark green canopy formed by cedar branches overhead. The conifer-perfumed air at ground level was still and sweet. Light breezes moved the trees' crowns high above. I grew captivated by the way they swayed close to one another but never quite touched, leaving intricate, constantly changing ribbons of sky in between. And I thought of ... nothing. And I did that for ... I don't know how long. I never slept, but when I got up I was filled with that morning feeling of waking to a fresh day.

My lie-down in the woods didn't prove a thing other than that I am perhaps a suggestible person. Yet science has been able to document connections between forest-bathing and healthful consequences. The question is, Why? Why should time in a green space or in touch with nature through other means be able to trigger a set of biochemical changes that can strengthen physical health and mental equilibrium? The answer to that goes back in time—way back.

The autonomic nervous system is present in vertebrates as a group. Virtually all modern species are outfitted with fight-or-flight and rest-and-relax responses that were being refined in fish and amphibians hundreds of millions of years ago.

Mammals have been around in one form or another for at least 150 million years. Their autonomic nervous systems were highly developed by the time the first primates arose 75 to 85 million years ago. Roughly the size of squirrels, these early forms are believed to have made their home in the trees

Forward-facing stereoscopic vision for gauging precise distances and nimble hands with opposable thumbs for grasping and manipulating objects are our inheritance from tree-dwelling ancestors dating back millions of years. Democratic Republic of the Congo.
CHRISTOPHE COURTEAU/MINDEN PICTURES

of tropical woodlands. When you've got dinosaurs ruling the ground—remember, they didn't disappear until around 65 million years ago—keeping to branches high off the ground seems like an excellent plan. Those were the environments that shaped the primate group's characteristics: stereoscopic vision (forward-facing eyes with fields of view that overlap to allow greater depth perception), good color discrimination (helpful in finding fruits), dexterous digits and opposable thumbs (for climbing and increasingly useful for manipulating objects), and bigger brains. We humans share the primate family's strong reliance on visual clues. And according to recent research, our sense of smell isn't as poor as is generally believed. It's just that much of our detection of odors takes place below the conscious level.

HUMAN EVOLUTION

bipedalistic hominids appear about 8 million years ago   *Australopithecus*

●●●●●●●●●●   ●●●●●●●●●●   ●●
          ●●●●●●●●●●   ●●●●●●●●●●
● = *100,000 years*

But let's swing forward to our particular family of mammals, the great apes, which branched off from the rest of the primates 13 to 15 million years ago. Like their predecessors, they inhabited lush woodlands—they, too, were forest-bathing throughout their lives. The earliest members of the hominid subfamily, distinguished in part by the habit of upright walking on two legs (bipedalism), may have separated from the other great apes as early as 7 to 8 million years ago. *Australopithecus* arose 3.5 to 4 million years ago. The first members of our genus, *Homo*, walked onto the scene about 2.8 million years back. Another 2.45 million years went by before *Homo sapiens*, modern humans, appeared 350,000 years ago.

Australopithecus
Aw-struh-low-pi-
thuh-kiss

If we convert the period from planet Earth's origin 4.5 to 4.7 billion years ago until now into a 24-hour day, the first life awakened before 4 and 5 a.m. The eukaryotes got going sometime before 10 in the morning. And modern humans walked into the scene seconds before midnight. But we do have a history, and

... start[ing] only 7 or 8 million years ago with the earliest hominids, we humans [have] spent 99.9 percent of our existence in natural settings.

Arthropocene epoch begins with the Industrial Revolution

Homo   *Homo sapien*

here's a different timescale to put it in perspective: The onset of the Industrial Revolution and rapid urbanization—considered by many to mark the start of the Anthropocene epoch—took place less than three centuries ago. If we look 75 to 85 million years back to the origin of primates as a starting point, then 99.99 percent of the evolution of our primate order of mammals was molded by natural surroundings. If we start only 7 or 8 million years ago with the earliest hominids, we humans still spent 99.9 percent of our existence in natural settings. During that time, hominids expanded into more open woodlands, savannas, and eventually, other habitats. But none of our early or more recent human ancestors experienced anything remotely equivalent to the sights, sounds, and demands of the environments most *Homo sapiens* dwell in today.

We are out of our element, increasingly removed from natural conditions and suddenly subject to an array of situations and stimuli that our evolution didn't prepare us for. This mismatch all too commonly generates anxiety and stress in daily life. When stress becomes chronic, this may lead to a weakening of the immune system, inflammation of tissues, depression, and other kinds of disease (dis-ease). In short, it can cause a variety of ailments of the type labeled noncommunicative diseases to distinguish them from illnesses caused by infections.

In a natural setting, you may be aware of saying to yourself: *Nice here. Kinda peaceful. Smells good too. Could the sweet fragrance I'm picking up be coming from those little blossoms over there by … ? Whoa, look at this gnarled old tree trunk … .* Subconsciously, though, your whole being is saying: *I'm home,* where your senses, nerves, glands, and flesh (and, for all we know, your microbiome) chorus, *This feels right.* The feeling is of belonging. It is older than you and lies deeper than you can reach with your conscious thoughts.

You've been immersed in nature since the chromosomes of your father's sperm joined those of your mother's egg.

A little contact with natural environments is healthy. More is healthier. Being involved with nature is not a particular choice, and it is not a hobby, as birdwatching or flower-gardening are often described. It is not any sort of special interest, the practice of a philosophy, or a concern best-suited to extrasensitive types, or to folks keen to preserve antique objects and historical sites, or even to hardcore outdoors enthusiasts. That's because having a relationship with nature is not optional. You've been immersed in nature since the chromosomes of your father's sperm joined those of your mother's egg. No matter what kind of activities or groups you identify with now, you stay profoundly involved with nature day and night because it built and selected the genes that in turn built you and the operating systems of your body and mind. Those systems respond to nature's presence, and they respond in more subtle but very real ways to its absence—to its replacement by modern settings and stimuli. There are no exceptions.

· · ·

Kids: Go ahead and get dirty. Tell your mom you're on a health kick. If you see from her expression that she's not buying your story, add that you're taking sensible precautions against developing allergies and possibly more serious diseases as an adult. To be honest, if you are old enough to read this, it's getting a little late. The best time to play in the dirt is as soon as you learn to crawl.

You have a marvelous immune system designed by near-countless generations of animal ancestors to become steadily stronger and more adaptable as you grow. It does this through repeated exposure to a varied array of microorganisms. You're full of professional little fighters—warrior cells like the lymphocytes swarming to attack microbes that have the potential to cause infection. In the process of destroying those enemies, the fighters, armed with molecular weapons, improve their abilities to recognize, disable, and overcome the same type of microbes during a future encounter.

If left unchallenged, the immune system may acquire only part of its potential and be more easily overwhelmed by a surprise invasion. A different problem arises when the system's warriors begin to attack a person's own cells, which can lead to lupus, celiac disease, inflammatory bowel disease, rheumatoid arthritis, psoriasis, or other conditions categorized as autoimmune disorders. The causes of such misdirected defensive activity are far from being thoroughly understood. However, some studies point to the possibility that, in some cases, autoimmune problems may be due to the absence of historically normal levels of assaults from parasites, bacteria, and viruses for your warrior cells to deal with. Like bored army soldiers in a bar starting a brawl with the civilians they're supposed to defend, your immune troopers turn to picking fights with healthy cells.

Research into the acute lymphoblastic form of childhood leukemia reveals an interesting parallel. This is the most frequent form of cancer in children and teens. One in twenty babies in the world is born with a common genetic mutation that predisposes the child to the disease. Kids whose immune systems are strengthened during the first year by plenty of exposure to microbes in the environment are at low risk of having this form of leukemia ever develop. By contrast, according to a 2018 research summary in the journal *Nature Reviews Cancer*, children reared in more sterile settings such as hyperhygienic modern homes (thoroughly scrubbed, often with antiseptic wipes and sprays) tend to have stunted immune systems. When one of these children catches a cold or flu, it can trigger a second mutation that leaves the young person more susceptible to lymphoblastic leukemia, according to the author, Mel Greaves from London's Institute of Cancer.

"The problem is not infection," Greaves said in an interview with *The Guardian*. "The problem is lack of infection." Which would explain why this type of leukemia remains rare to absent in many developing nations, where household hygiene is often minimal, yet is increasingly common in affluent countries. Greaves thinks it's possible that poor early development of the immune system due to overly sanitized living conditions might also be related to the onset of Hodgkin's lymphoma, type 1 diabetes, multiple sclerosis, and any number of allergies.

Even putting aside our hordes of microbial partners and the way our autonomic nervous systems and immune systems function, we are shaped by nature from our furred heads to our toes—still mobile enough to partially curl around a slender branch—and from the umbilical cord connection on our front side to the stubby tailbone at the rear. Part of our brain may tell us something else, insisting that we are not constrained by the past, that we can do or be anything we want to. There is plenty of truth to this claim, but it doesn't change the fact that each of us is physically a natural product from the fertilized egg onward and responds accordingly, despite anything we choose to think instead. As I said earlier, the human heartbeat and blood chemistry don't lie. Neither does your immune system, and neither does your DNA.

. . .

All of us might do well to reappraise who and what we are by nature and think more about the effects of the habitats we are fashioning for ourselves today. And I don't mean just in terms of microbes and immune systems. The great ape line of primates gave rise to hominins, the ancestral line of humans, between 4 and 5 million years ago. *Homo sapiens* branched off from those earlier humans 350,000 years ago. And up until 6,000 years ago, 0 percent of our species inhabited anything that could be called an urban area. As late as the year 1800 AD, only 6 percent did. By the mid-twentieth century, 30 percent did. Scarcely seventy years after that, meaning right now, 55 percent of humanity occupies urban areas. Two-thirds to three-quarters of the global population is expected to be urban by 2050. For most developed nations, the figure is already around 75 percent. In a number of countries, including some less developed ones, one-tenth to more than one-half of the total population is clustered in a single megacity.

According to the World Health Organization, air, water, and soil pollution, together with chemical exposure, climate change, and other factors associated with altered environments, now claim the lives of about 12.6 million people annually. That represents nearly one of every four human deaths from all sources. The single largest environmental health risk facing humankind is air pollution. It is a leading cause of chronic obstructive pulmonary diseases, acute respiratory infections, cardiovascular problems, and cancers, and it is worst in urban areas. While news headlines keep our attention on armed conflicts around the globe, we overlook the fact that the count of people dying yearly from air pollution alone, between 8 and 9 million, is three times the toll from wars (counting civilian casualties), malaria, AIDS, and tuberculosis combined.

In a 2001 survey, the US Environmental Protection Agency found that Americans are inside buildings 87 percent of the time and on average spend another 6 percent of their time in an automobile or some other enclosed mode of transportation. In other words, for 93 percent of their moments on Earth, typical Americans are voluntarily confined within various shells of our own making.

This is not to say that, by itself, being indoors that much makes people less happy or healthy than they might be otherwise. But it isn't the lifestyle our bodies and minds are adapted for. Fully 80 percent of adults in this nation don't meet the minimum public health guidelines for physical activity. It's probably not just poor eating habits that explain why more than four in ten Americans qualify as obese. Nor is it likely that social and economic pressures are the sole reason anxiety, depression, and other psychiatric disorders now afflict one in every five American adults. (If the number of cases that go unreported were included, mental health experts say, the percentage would be substantially higher.) And it's almost certainly more than just bad luck that after rising for decades, Americans' life expectancy has declined in recent years due in large part to a combination of increasing obesity, drug overdoses, alcohol-related diseases, and suicides.

Aw crap. I made a pledge to stay away from alarming statistics, and, sure enough, here I am, piling them up again. But here we all are—at a stage in human history where nearly 8 billion of us are engaged in a wholesale denaturing of the planet, creating less hospitable environments for ourselves while defining what we're doing as progress. The farther we continue in this direction, the harder we are working against our own best interests as well as those of our fellow Earthlings. Knowing what we know now, it would be good for a species that named itself *sapiens*—Latin for "wise"—to start choosing smarter paths forward. If we can quit congratulating ourselves for being exceptional creatures long enough to embrace a more realistic vision of what human nature actually is, that would count as a very promising and much healthier change of trajectory.

To position any of this as a moral issue—old-time environments good, modern environments bad; nature noble and uplifting, cities cramped and dispiriting—is to make a hash out of valuable scientific findings. The stimulating, productive, creative, socially rewarding aspects of living in urban areas are enormous. And it's true as well that going to the outdoors some days might net you little but foul weather, annoying bugs, treacherous terrain, and exhaustion. Whenever our ancient forbears left a campsite or shelter to travel or forage, they didn't go out into a natural setting. They never left a natural setting, since everyplace was wild. They may have been forest-bathing or savanna-bathing like crazy, yet they also had to be on the lookout for biting insects; venomous snakes; large, fierce predators; and hoofed and horned wildlife that was faster and stronger than humans—not to mention unfriendly neighboring bands or tribes.

What proved valuable to hominid survival and well-being through the ages wasn't the fight-or-flight sympathetic nervous system or the easy-does-it parasympathetic system but the combination of the two. That is why we modern humans ended up with this time-tested duality, and now face the challenge of operating with it in modern environments. The solution in the past was not to favor one system over the other, and it is not the solution today. The thing to focus on is restoring a health-giving balance between them.

. . .

What can one person do? Bend, stretch, dance, bike, paddle, climb, hike, run, jog, walk, or just mosey ... but *move*, however you are able. One medical study after another has demonstrated the striking benefits of even modest exercise in reducing the most common health risks: obesity, high blood pressure, heart disease, diabetes, and depression. In a 2019 *Journal of the American Medical Association (JAMA) Internal Medicine* publication, the authors reported that older women who averaged 4,400 steps per day (a bit over two miles) had a 41 percent lower risk of death than those who averaged 2,700. The risk of death continued to decline up to 7,500 steps, which is still no more than one good walk combined with normal daily activities.

Combining our inherited tree-climbing skills with human inventiveness, a Ba-Benzélé pygmy carries smoky leaves to stun bees while gathering honey a hundred feet above a rainforest floor in the Democratic Republic of the Congo.
MICHAEL NICHOLS

A 2016 *JAMA Internal Medicine* paper presented results from twelve studies of a total of 1.44 million people aged nineteen to ninety-eight who had no history of cancer. Those with the highest rate of leisure-time physical activity proved to have a 20 percent lower risk of getting any of seven types of cancer and a 10 to 20 percent lower risk of developing six other types. And the physical activity involved was low-intensity exercise, not strenuous athletics. Equally important, other studies have

shown how moderate exercise increases cognitive abilities including mental alertness, learning, problem-solving, and memory. The hippocampus is the region of the brain most involved in memory formation. It begins to shrink in older adults as part of the normal aging process. However, in a group of older test subjects who walked around a track for forty minutes per day three times a week, that shrinkage did more than just come to a halt. It reversed. At the end of one year, the

The green rooftop sprouting atop Chicago's city hall showcases a way to dampen the urban heat island effect of buildings and capture carbon dioxide. It boasts 20,000 plants, including trees, as well as honey-producing beehives. MARK MAHANEY/REDUX

participants' hippocampus had grown an average of 2 percent in volume.

So, yes, move, move, move. We're designed for it. And do this outdoors in touch with nature whenever possible. We're deep-down designed for that too. The results from forest-bathing (or hanging out in as much greenery as you have handy) overlap in so many ways with those from exercise that it's like doubling up on the health benefits. Do it. We all want a strong, alert, healthy, and long life. I don't know a surer way to achieve that.

What can one person do beyond that? You might start by planting a tree or two somewhere or a little garden, if only in a windowsill box. Move on to working with local authorities and organizing volunteers to create a small green neighborhood park. Or two. Then support county open-space bonds that compensate rural landowners for placing conservation easements on their property in order to maintain some of its natural character. Maybe go on to lobby for protecting a chunk of the nearest intact backcountry as wildland. And consider supporting one of the groups working internationally to conserve natural habitats and stymie the massive trade in illegal wildlife. Take care of nature, take care of yourself, take care of humankind. Same deal in the long run. These are not either/or choices.

Campaigning to fend off the latest heedless development to threaten an area's environmental quality and rushing from one species in crisis to the next are worthy efforts that save good places and wild lives. Yet they are emergency actions, and they are being overwhelmed by the Anthropocene forces putting many more natural settings and wild communities in jeopardy hourly. The good news is that other modern forces are combining to build a strategy for changing that pattern. Holistic approaches to health, alternative technologies, the global exchange of information, social media, and growing attention to human and animal rights all spread awareness of the rapidly deteriorating global environment and the importance of restoring balance. If that can be combined with a rethinking of what the true nature of nature is and how it encompasses our greater selves—who knows? Modern civilization and this resilient and old planet might even make friends and go on to prosper together.

NEXT SPREAD

The beauty and moods of forests take many forms that in some places come lit by natural magic—the bioluminescence of fireflies. TIM FLACH

Elephants and Excavations

There are places in Africa's eastern and southern savanna regions that harbor assemblies of creatures so grand and abundant, so strong, swift, striped, spotted, maned, horned, and fanged, that it's easy to imagine the Age of Mammals never gave way to the Anthropocene. The air smells of freshly chewed and trampled vegetation, dung and urine, musky secretions, and sun-warmed hides. At times, whole horizons appear to be on the move. This is a zootic landscape—a setting defined and constantly shaped and reshaped by big untamed beasts, where the tracks you leave on the ground join a primeval mosaic of hoofprints, pawprints, and intersecting animal trails among fresh diggings and bones.

Though my own home lies amid forested mountains in the Rockies, part of me always wants to be back on an African plain where animals remain a dominant physical presence in the

environment. Maybe the fact that Africa's mix of open wood-lands and savannas is where my kind—*sapiens* kind—arose has something to do with the way those settings tug at me.

As I looked round the Kenyan countryside one day, I gave some extra thought to what my early ancestors might have been busy with in that terrain eons before. What I was doing was clinging to a roll bar in the back of a truck as it bounced and swayed at full speed along a dirt track. My companions were part of a patrol unit in a national park. We had been inspect-ing the gruesome evidence of operations by *shifta*, the name for

As the largest land mammals, elephants, as adults, are virtually immune to predators and very effective at protecting their more vulnerable young.
MICHAEL NICHOLS

Savanna elephants are a different species than forest elephants (like the male shown here), yet both have suffered devastating losses from poachers seeking ivory tusks to sell.
MICHAEL NICHOLS

well-armed bandits from neighboring Somalia (or sometimes Ethiopia) who came here to raid ivory by turning live elephants into dead ones.

Several of the corpses we found were recent. Earlier targets, withered into mummified sheets of hide streaked with vulture shit, lay on soil stained black by blood and putrefying internal fluids. All of the victims had their trunks hacked off and their faces torn apart where the poachers removed the elongated incisor teeth—the tusks. I remember that someone's handset radio crackled, and a series of shouted sentences in Swahili came through the speaker. All at once, everybody in our group was yelling and running for the truck. And we were off; where to or why, I had no idea.

In 2016, the Kenyan government set ablaze 105 tons of illegally taken elephant tusks and rhinoceros horn to emphasize the nation's determination to shut down the illegal killing that threatened its wildlife heritage—and its tourism industry.
BEN CURTIS/AP

There were several of us standing shoulder to shoulder on the truck's bed, dodging the thorny acacia branches whipping past in places. Unable to understand Swahili, I gathered from snippets translated for me that we were racing to check out a fresh report of poachers in the area. Bullets were being fired somewhere up ahead. Scanning the surroundings, I forgot to duck, and paid for it with a whack from an acacia branch. My first thought was that I'd been shot, and I was thrilled to realize an instant later that the blood on my head was only from thorns.

I'd been told by park guards about *shifta* dressing in camouflage fatigues mimicking the uniforms of patrol forces in the area—Anti-Poaching Units (APUs), made up of local park scouts and Kenya Wildlife Service rangers, and General Service Units (GSUs), formed from police or army personnel brought in as reinforcements. There had been incidents when the *shifta* attempted to lead GSU or APU groups into an ambush, and one real screwup where GSU and APU patrols began firing toward each other in the confusion.

I wished I knew what the hell our immediate plan was. Mostly, I wished I had a weapon, not to take part in any assault but to have a hope of discouraging someone with a weapon intent on poaching me. I'd been given rifles to carry elsewhere in Africa while reporting on wildlife. In one remote reserve plagued by guerilla activities, I'd ridden in vehicles with armored plates under the seats, put there to limit injuries if we hit any of the land mines planted in the dirt roads. I'd had to deal with more land mines on jungle trails I hiked while looking for Asian elephants. And I once came unarmed upon nervous elephant poachers in a stretch of African jungle so remote that they could have killed me with little risk of ever getting caught. They looked like they were considering just that, until they realized no one in my little group showed any interest in learning their identity. While I'm sure early hominids faced plenty of challenges, you know you're in the Anthropocene when the threats include gunpowder, steel snares, and an international trade in illegal wildlife products whose profits rival those from the underground trafficking of weapons, drugs, and human beings.

The frenzy of ivory poaching in the 1980s, spurred largely by demand from Japan, the United States, and booming economies in Southeast Asia, was stifled by an international ban on the trade in tusks in 1990. During the present century, the ban was partially lifted, and a second wave of elephant slaughter swept Africa as the price of ivory soared again, this time fueled mainly by demand from China. That nation's economy had grown to a level rivaling America's, creating an enormous new class of consumers who wanted luxury items to display their wealth. After international pressure finally persuaded China to announce that it would end ivory trading within its borders at the end of 2017, the price for tusks fell quickly from its high of nearly $1,000 per pound to half that amount.

Yet black market ivory remains valuable enough that the carnage continues in a number of countries. Adding to the mayhem are insurgent and terrorist groups selling tusks to fund their operations. In addition to the take of elephants, some poachers poison waterholes, which also ends the life of every other animal that comes to drink.

Illegal trade in rhinoceros horn meanwhile keeps heavy pressure on Africa's second-largest mammal, the white rhino. The last male in the northern subspecies just died in 2018. Africa's black rhinos are critically endangered. India's one-horned rhinos are also besieged by poaching and habitat loss. So are Sumatran rhinos, now thought to number fewer than 100 in the wild. And the population of the fifth and final species, the Javan rhino, is estimated at no more than sixty. Even where surviving rhinos in Africa are closely attended around the clock by guards, raiders have at times swept in and executed both the animals and their protectors.

I have no exciting finale for the story of rushing to capture elephant poachers that day years ago in Kenya. By the time we arrived on the scene, the *shifta* had hightailed it to a stretch of adjoining woodland and melted back into the bush. That some members of our species are perfectly content to carry out genocide on another species and become all the more eager to do it as an animal's scarcity subsequently raises the value of its teeth, horns, glands, or fur—or its penis in the case of the big wild cats—is part of the endless puzzle of human value systems.

If a 13,000-pound male African savanna elephant falls riddled with bullets so its tusks can be cut into little ivory trinkets, there are millions of shoppers who apparently couldn't care less as long as they can display one of those baubles as a status symbol. At the same time, growing numbers of people around the world are willing to spend a substantial sum just to behold such animals alive and roaming free. And many people who may never travel to where elephants survive nevertheless send personal funds to conservation groups for saving those largest of all land mammals. The most thought-provoking puzzle pieces are the members of our species willing to go into the field and dedicate their lives to protecting other kinds of creatures there, even when they know they may get murdered for trying.

. . .

A lot of Westerners still think of sub-Saharan Africa in general as a realm filled with spectacular wildlife in between villages. That vision gets reinforced by the images in magazines, movies, and television specials while in reality, large native animals are becoming hard to find across much of the region. Countries with the least corruption, most stable governments, and well-managed international support for conservation efforts have the best chances for countering organized poaching. However, nearly every sub-Saharan nation in Africa faces an equal challenge of protecting its native fauna from the consequences of rapid human population growth: a thriving bushmeat trade, subsistence hunting with guns and wire snares, the killing of predators that threaten the security of people and their livestock, and the conflicts that arise from wild herbivores eating crops as their former range is replaced by expanding agriculture. As of 2018, the average number of humans per square mile stood at 4 in Canada, 93 in the United States, 308 in France, and 390 in China. Malawi had many more: 526 people per square mile. Gambia had 554, Nigeria 557, and Uganda 574, while Rwanda houses 1,312 per square mile, a higher population density than India.

Despite mounting problems and pressures, quite a few African reserves still offer escape-from-time vistas where you can judge the hour

POPULATION DENSITY

• = 10 people per square mile

Rwanda
Uganda
Nigeria
Gambia
Malawi
China
France
United States
Canada

of the day by the sun but can't tell from your surroundings which century you're in. Before I ever heard of forest-bathing, on some days during an expedition deep into the green profusion of central Africa's tropical rainforest, I almost felt like I was forest-drowning. In the continent's eastern plains and southern velds, I found myself again in the middle of all the wild I could absorb, surrounded by many-hued tons of big animal life. Herds of gazelles, zebras, and wildebeest grazed side by side, passing elephants that curled the ends of their trunks around bunches of grass to pull up whole sheaves at a time, while giraffes stood stripping leaves from tree branches two stories above.

An aerial view of a zootic savanna landscape being patterned by its biggest foragers, tramplers, and trumpeting raisers of dust. Sudd, Sudan.
GEORGE STEINMETZ

But if a full-blown safari isn't your thing, that's OK. You can still get benefits by getting your hands on a critter. Much as with forest-bathing, petting or playing with a pet or other animal companion can bring about a lowering of blood pressure, a reduction of cholesterol and fat-building triglyceride levels, and a decrease in anxiety together with increases in the feel-good neurotransmitter dopamine and the mood-stabilizing neurotransmitter serotonin. Positive physiological responses also occur in subjects shown pictures of scenery that they describe as instilling a sense of awe and wonder. Viewing photos from Africa's plains certainly meets that standard. Being there in person never fails to crank up the amazement dosage for me, no matter how many days in a row I spend beholding a savanna's moving wardrobe of fauna.

Sooner or later, though, my thoughts turn toward trying to understand how a drought-prone plain stippled with patches of brush and trees is able to support so many large creatures in such splendid variety. Elephants always draw the eye first. In the course of their foraging, the ones I followed uprooted shrubs to eat, broke down whole tree limbs to get at the leaves, fruits, or

ELEPHANTS AND EXCAVATIONS

nuts, and stripped off so much tasty bark from some of the larger trees that they girdled them. Together with wildfire, these gray titans become a major ecological force keeping the woodlands that tend to encroach upon savannas in check.

Depending on its size, an adult elephant will consume 250 to 400-plus pounds of vegetation per day. Which means that each day at least 150 to 300 pounds of rich fertilizer—reprocessed plant cells and fibers loaded with microbes, leftover digestive juices, and other organic material—is going to come out the other end. The stuff smells like sour hay or something you discovered too late in the back of your fridge, but it's not terribly off-putting. Certain large nuts pass through elephants intact. Emulating a local biologist I was in the field with at the time, I dug into dung piles to pick the nuts out, cracked open the shells, and ate the seeds inside. They tasted fine.

I'd watched baboons take nuts, hard berries, and partially digested fruits from the dung. Ground hornbills do that too. My biologist companion looked healthy enough, but as a newbie myself in the business of rummaging through elephant turds for a snack, I still found it reassuring to learn that the hornbills live to be fifty years old or more. Finches and starlings also pecked at the piles, though I couldn't always tell whether they were going after seeds or insects attracted to the droppings. In heavily forested areas, even the knee-high antelope called duikers scavenge partly digested fruits from elephant droppings.

Hundreds of different species of dung beetles, part of the scarab family, inhabit a typical African savanna. Many follow scents to a fragrant mess of elephant poo and start feasting like starving vegetarians on a mountainside of stewed spinach (though close-up observations show some of these beetles

dining mainly on films of fungi and broths of bacteria among the plant matter). Others excavate soil beneath the pile to move some of the dung down to a more secure spot underground, where the female deposits eggs and the emerging larvae can grow amid a ready store of food. Still other dung beetles remove material from the mound atop the ground, form it into a ball ranging in size from a pea to a grapefruit, depending on how big the breed of beetle is, and roll it away some distance to a spot of soft ground. There the rollers bury the ball—as deep as three feet in the case of the largest beetles (*Heliocopris*). The

With elephants and native hoofed animals hunted out and wild habitats replaced by farmland and pastures, the dung beetles in the Lake Albert area of Uganda now make use of horse manure.
JOEL SARTORE

Heliocopris
He-lee-oh-cop-ris

adults of some species lay only a single egg and may remain in an underground chamber to defend the offspring and the food stash. This strategy is effective against other burrowing invertebrates. It isn't much help, however, when the predator is a long-clawed honey badger in the habit of sniffing out buried dung beetle nests and digging down like a hyperactive mini-backhoe to get at the plump grubs.

Elephants distribute a variety of plants simply by traveling widely and depositing seeds in droppings across the countryside. The efforts of countless dung beetles to store the stuff underground amount to what a gardener would do: plant seeds at depth in enriched composting material after loosening the soil, aerating it, and making it more permeable to water. While the ball-rolling beetles are distributing the elephant dung bonanza, the activities of other creatures extend the effect still farther. Flies and other insects feeding on the excrement will produce rich droppings of their own after they move off, and the birds and mammals picking through the elephant poo are likely to scatter droppings that contain seeds as well as fertilizer.

Similar networks of dispersal for plants and nutrients operate around the dung of rhinos and hippos, which repeatedly defecate in certain sites, creating impressive mounds thought to be markers of territory or dominance. Antelope such as steenbok, several kinds of gazelles, and the graceful little dik-diks also make these territorial middens. Almost every herbivore and every carnivore has grateful dung beetles spreading its droppings around somewhere. Wherever death overtakes one of the savanna's large mammals, the scavenger community of hyenas, jackals, foxes, and vultures sets to work carrying off scraps and leaving their feces with concentrated nutrients over a wider area.

While some dung beetle species make use of scavengers' droppings around a carcass, an array of other insect species will be feeding and breeding on the carrion or hauling morsels off to hives or burrows until the corpse is almost completely decomposed. African porcupines, protected by quills more than a foot long, may show up at a carcass, sometimes to eat carrion but more typically to gnaw on the bones for minerals long after other scavengers have finished. This is not natural history at its most picturesque, but no savanna would flourish as it does without everybody large and small, majestic or scuttling around doing things humans consider pretty disgusting, spreading the organic wealth around and cycling it back into the soil.

. . .

Another way elephants influence the habitats and lives of other species in savanna ecosystems is by using their tusks, trunk, and feet for excavating holes to a depth where enough groundwater collects in the bottom for a drink. Typically, African plains are semiarid landscapes with annual rainy seasons followed by longer parched seasons, and they are subject to cycles of drought that may last for years. During dry spells, the availability of these elephant-made wells can become an important factor in the survival of other fauna in the region. The wells were probably important to our hominid ancestors too, both as reserves of water and magnets for prey.

Ecologists refer to an animal that plays a pivotal role in wildlife communities as a keystone species. Elephants are a hard-to-miss example. Lions qualify as a keystone species as well, for as the top predators in the savanna community, they exert an outsize influence on the whereabouts, behavior, and numbers of herbivores. I

think that as a group, the dung beetles deserve a keystone title as well. Yet even with the continual enrichment of soils by these six-legged recyclers, you wonder how the vegetation holds up month after month and year after year under the grazing and browsing pressure of so many mouths, especially during drought periods when powdery dust rises from the slightest shuffle of a hoof.

Like other tropical and subtropical ecosystems, African plains largely escaped the dramatic changes caused by glacial advances and retreats at other latitudes. Native plants on the savannas co-evolved with the animals eating them in a comparatively steady environment for millions of years. The outcome was more

A lion stalks an alert Grant's zebra in the tall grasses of Kenya's Maasai Mara National Reserve, which adjoins Tanzania's famed Serengeti National Park.
TONY CROCETTA/ BIOSPHOTO/ MINDEN PICTURES

and more specialization of niches—more fine-tuning of who feeds on what, where, and when. Each variety of herbivore on those wild pastures may be selecting a different combination of vegetation, depending on that animal's tolerance for tough plant tissues, spiky growths, distasteful substances, or harsher toxins the plants produce to discourage diners. Of course, much depends on the particular mix of gut microbes each type of animal harbors to digest different fibers and neutralize the plants' chemical defenses.

Where several grazing species rely on the same grasses and herbs, they may focus on different parts or stages of growth, just as the browsing species that favor woody plants select different portions of the bushes (slender branch tips, thicker branches, buds, tender young leaves, older leaves, flowers, fruits, etc.) for meals or dine at different heights. Despite this segregation of feeding patterns, the pressure from hungry herbivores does get severe at times. Yet savanna vegetation is well adapted to tolerate both heavy use and drought conditions. And the animals that depend on those plants are well adapted to get the most nourishment possible out of dried-up stalks and leaves that sometimes offer little more than cellulose, the basic structural fiber of vegetation. Vertebrates can't digest cellulose on their own. They rely on the help of gut microbes that not only break down cellulose but can also rework its chemistry to create nutrients valuable to their host in the process.

An especially close living relationship that has evolved between two organisms of different species is called a *symbiosis*. The definition includes relationships that are predatory, parasitic, or cases of freeloading, with one organism plainly gaining more than the other from an association. However, the term symbiosis is most often used to describe a true partnership, or mutualism, with each of the participants (termed *symbionts*) reaping strong benefits from the arrangement. The hoofed animals known as ruminants have complex, four-chambered stomachs that perform a sequence of different tasks. On balance, the most important function of the ruminant digestive system is providing prime habitat for communities of symbiotic microbes that can convert forage into vitamins, fatty acids, amino acids, and other nourishing chemical compounds.

After chewing and swallowing plant material, a ruminant first sends it through two stomach chambers that are essentially fermentation vats. There, mixed with saliva and other liquids, the food becomes covered in bacteria, archaea, yeasts, other fungi, and protists, many of them busy deconstructing cellulose's complex carbohydrates and multiplying like mad. Then the animal regurgitates the results to begin grinding the fibers again with its teeth and adding more saliva—chewing the cud—before sending what are now smaller, softer food particles back to the fermentation vats for a second round of major microbial munching.

Next, the slurry passes to a third chamber, where water is absorbed, then on to the fourth chamber, where gastric juices and enzymes break down the food particles further and also start to digest the throngs of nutrient-packed microbes and their rich byproducts. Digestion and absorption continue all the way through the fourth and last stomach chamber and on through the lengthy small intestine. Finally, the slurry moves into the large intestine, where water and still more nutrients are extracted and passed into the animal's circulatory system until what's left of the meal reaches the tail end of the digestive tract and drops back onto the savanna. Of course, if you're a dung beetle in the vicinity, these "waste products" are manna falling from the heavens and destined for yet another round of dining by you and the microbial guests in your own beetle model of a digestive system.

Now, underneath the dusty, trampled, chewed-over, crapped-on, beetle-burrowed cover of grasses and herbs on the ground are lush root systems spreading widely from each cluster of stalks and penetrating deep enough to tap moisture from ten or even twenty feet down. As much as 80 percent of a perennial grass's weight consists of such fibrous roots. And their reach within the soil is multiplied by the other major mutualism that helps explain animal richness on an African plain: networks of symbiotic fungus threads that attach to almost every grass's underground portion.

mycorrhiza
my-kor-ree-zuh

mycorrhizae
my-kor-rai-zee

Known as a *mycorrhiza* (plural: *mycorrhizae*), each individual fungus strand wraps around a root hair to colonize either its surface or the cells inside and grows outward through the soil. Together, the strands of multiple mycorrhizae form an immense secondary branching root system. If you were to dig down, expecting to have a look for yourself, you wouldn't see most of this remarkable plant partnership because the fungal filaments are smaller than small. The dirt caught in the tread on the bottom of your shoe alone may hold dozens of miles of these microscopic mycorrhizae; a spadeful of dirt holds many hundreds of miles. Like roots, the threads transport water, minerals, and other nutrients from the surrounding soil to the plant. But since a mycorrhiza is able to meander among the soil granules through mini-spaces not even the finest root hair could penetrate, the fungal network may be harvesting raw materials from an area ten or more times greater than the root system could draw from by itself. The fungi also produce enzymes and acids able to break down certain minerals more efficiently than the plant roots could. In return for their efforts, the mycorrhizae receive a reliable supply of the sugars and starches produced by their host's aboveground parts through photosynthesis.

People tend to associate fungi with damp, musty conditions. But mycorrhizae are common in nearly every environment, and they form symbiotic associations with most of the herbs, shrubs, and trees in an area as well as with the grasses there. In semi-arid lands, these invisible probing threads become all the more important in extracting water. On an African plain, as elsewhere, many of what we see as separate bunches of grass are clones that spread by underground stems, or rhizomes. And the members of a clone can share nutrients with one another via their

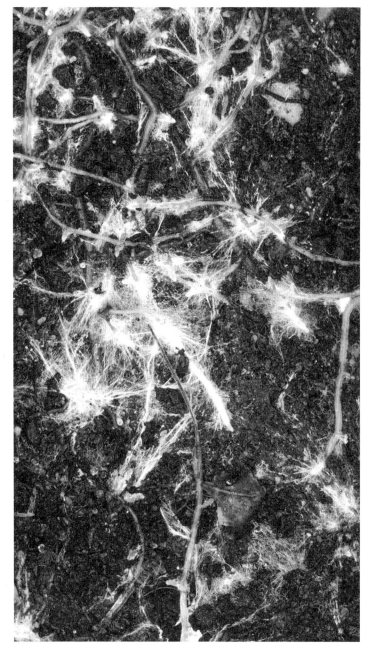

About 90 percent of all plants form mutually beneficial—symbiotic— associations with root fungi known as mycorrhizae. The fungal threads deliver water and nutrients from a far greater area than the roots themselves can reach. JEREMY BURGESS/SCIENCE PHOTO LIBRARY

ELEPHANTS AND EXCAVATIONS

mycorrhizal network and through their root systems. One grass clone may exchange nutrients with a separate clone of the same species. The mycorrhizal filigree can also connect plants of different species and even different families of vegetation.

Picture a newly sprouted grass or herb struggling to grow in a patch of poor savanna soil. To build tissues and chlorophyll, the seedling needs nitrogen, but there may be none available from dung, urine, or reprocessed carcasses in that spot. Once the seedling hooks up with the mycorrhizal network, though, it can get nitrogen from grasses or herbs growing in more fertile spots. And if part of that same network also connects to the roots of a nearby acacia tree or at least probes the soil nearby, the seedling could have even better luck tapping into a lode of nitrogen compounds. The nitrogen bounty is not produced by the acacia itself but by symbiotic bacteria housed in nodules on the tree's roots. Like other plants in the legume (pea and bean) family, acacias specialize in hosting nitrogen-fixing bacteria—a group with the unique ability to capture nitrogen gas from the air. The microbes convert it to ammonia, which can then be incorporated into organic compounds used to build plant tissues and pigments. Grow, little seedling. Go for the sky.

. . .

Many plants form symbioses with several different species of mycorrhizal fungi, often at the same time. The plants also host other types of fungi and a spectrum of bacteria aboveground—just as we and other animals do with a variety of microbes. I've got to ask: Where in all this is a truly individual life form? Is there such a thing? Not really; not among organisms larger than those microbes. We all qualify as composite creatures.

We're not merely symbionts but communities of symbionts. A more accurate term for what we really are would be *holobionts*— assemblages of partners. I suppose we could even be viewed as ecosystems consisting of multiple smaller, interacting ecological units, which is the more technical description of a holobiont.

holobiont
holo-by-ont

If these definitions sound somewhat confusing, it's partly because biologists are still figuring out exactly how to talk about the implications of recent advances in their field. Previous generations worked diligently to sort the world's creatures into separate species. These were thought of as the fundamental units of life, somewhat like atoms were once considered the basic, indivisible particles of matter. Then, physicists found atoms to be collections of electrons, protons, and neutrons. Newer, more powerful instruments smashed those subatomic particles into smithereens, revealing sub-subatomic particles, and so on. Similarly, biologists keep uncovering consortiums of organisms—symbiotic partners, symbionts within those symbionts—tied intimately and consistently to what had earlier been thought of as single, discrete species.

NEXT SPREAD

For elephants—which can eat 200 to 600 pounds of food and drink up to 50 gallons of water per day— riverine habitats and swamplands become lifesaving habitat during dry seasons and more serious droughts.
GEORGE STEINMETZ

To analyze things literally means to take them apart, the better to understand what they are made of and how those pieces work. Biologists made great strides in analyses through the years, splitting nature into more precise categories in order to study those in greater detail. Now the results are beginning to tell us that perhaps further progress lies in the direction of synthesis—putting the pieces together, the better to understand how they function as a whole. While the traditional schemes for classifying life forms still prove convenient for many purposes, they are becoming less and less meaningful in other ways. Is that a problem? No; more like an awakening.

Daydreaming at the Fair

An African plain may be showier than other landscapes at the big-animal level, but as with any land-based ecosystem, the majority of its life forms and the majority of their interactions are hidden from ordinary view. If only we could see them more clearly. By sheer luck, I happen to know of a contraption that will allow us to do that right here. Except for the fact that the hub of this device is set at ground level, the thing looks like any other big, gaudily colored, carnival-style Ferris wheel you might find sitting out on a remote African savanna. In other words, it's completely make-believe. But don't let that stop you. The sign at the entrance—Ride the Great Circle of Life—welcomes one and all. And all you need is your imagination.

So, step in, buckle up, and you'll start rising above the grasses until you are looking down at the backs of the resident mammals going about their lives. As you ascend alongside an acacia tree,

you notice that it shades a couple of snoozing hyenas. When active, they will advertise their sex and reproductive readiness by pasting vegetation with chemical secretions from glands below their anus. Not that you're frantic to learn more about hyena stink, but the scent itself is manufactured by symbiotic bacteria thriving in those glands. Which counts as one of the many facts you'd need your imagination to picture even if you weren't along on this ride.

A circular view of the life and migrations that are so much a part of the Serengeti.
ALBERTO GHIZZI PANIZZA/ BIOSPHOTO/ MINDEN PICTURES

In another symbiosis, the whistling thorn acacia tree grows sugary nectaries to feed resident ants and hollow thorns to house them. In return, the ants attack any insects or larger animals attempting to eat the acacia's leaves. MARK MOFFETT/MINDEN PICTURES

The turning wheel soon brings you right next to the acacia's branches. Take an extra-close look. They are pimpled with little bud-like growths specialized to produce sugary sap. Ants are everywhere feeding on these structures, called nectaries. Notice how some of the tree's thorns grow noticeably larger than others and are hollow as well. The acacia produces these to house the ants. The ant colony's aggressive attacks on invaders threatening its homes and food sources become the acacia's solution for protecting itself from leaf-eating insects and larger herbivores undeterred by the normal spines. One symbiosis involves another here, for bacteria living within the ants' bodies produce antibiotics that these insects track across the acacia leaf

Vitelline masked weavers are widespread in Africa. After the male laces grass and reeds into the shape of a hanging ball, the female will line this nest's interior with soft feathers before laying her eggs.
TUI DE ROY/
MINDEN PICTURES

surfaces, thus defending the tree against harmful types of bacteria and fungi.

Weavers, shrikes, and a pair of blue cranes wing by. Soon, you're up far enough up to have your own bird's-eye view and make out the patterns of plant communities and animal trails, one with a lion pride padding along it. Along the nearby course of a shallow stream, a pool shimmers with reflected sunlight and ripples from the impala drinking at the edges. Viewed from the highest part of the ride, the larger contours of the landscape reveal themselves, enabling you to grasp how the distribution of plants and big animals changes with variations in the topography and the courses of the watershed. Then you begin to arc back down past the tops of other trees—a jackalberry and a marula, whose fruits have eight times the vitamin C of oranges—down past a colony of weaver birds' nests, several vervet monkeys perched on the same thick branch, a bush baby, a couple of tree hyraxes, an elephant shrew that has left its usual haunts on the ground and climbed up among the tree branches in its search for insects, and lithe lizards scrambling along the more slender branches. From there, you descend past the tallest bushes and the sturdy earthbound animals walking by, until you're back at the level of grasses, herbs, plant litter, dung, foraging ground ants and termites, shed fur, bones, stones ... the savanna's surface.

A cross-section reveals the crowded yet super-efficient construction of a termite nest, which may hold up to several million members. In East Africa, these tiny recyclers of vegetation outweigh all the wild animals on the surface combined.
CHRISTIAN ZIEGLER

But you don't stop, you don't even pause, for you're only halfway through the ecosystem. Being supernatural, this Ferris wheel ride brings you on into the topsoil (I'm still working out the imaginary details), which we think of as solid ground but is in fact a porous jungle of roots pocked with the burrows of small mammals and monitor lizards, aardvark-dug holes, dung beetle excavations, and corridors of the ant and termite colonies' nests. As you look more closely, you don't find less wildlife than you were seeing aboveground. You find more. It's just smaller, like the myriad of mites, millipedes, worms, and root-boring insect larvae that appear.

To see even more closely at this stage, you put on your special Great Circle of Life ultra-magnifying goggles (still working on that, too) so you can make out the tens of thousands of tiny arthropods called springtails inhabiting each cubic foot of soil and marvel at the intricate fabric of mycorrhizae woven among the soil granules. You wheel by the type of sticky fungal threads that lasso nematode worms for meals (which sounds purely imaginary but isn't) and on past mycorrhizae wrapping around

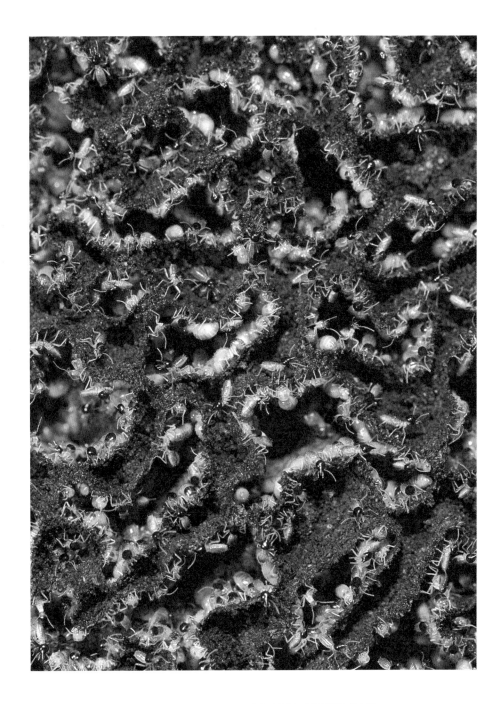

colonies of bacteria, absorbing the nutrients they exude and stockpiling carbon. Don't even bother trying to estimate numbers this far down, for there are many billions of bacteria representing thousands of species in each square foot of soil you roll by. Dirt is often dismissed as mostly inanimate debris. But you can now see how the stuff is more alive than dead. Even the sections of rock you pass are stuffed with countless microbes in the crevices.

Wherever you look, mobs of microorganisms are wriggling, stretching, eating, excreting, sequestering more carbon, synthesizing organic molecules, and releasing them at death for others to take up. By the time you ascend through the upside-down

CHAPTER SEVEN

forest of roots to the surface again, you'll understand how the community of life can be thicker, more varied, and a lot busier underground than the captivating communities of big plants and animals on the surface.

Nutrients accumulate aboveground, passed from little life forms to become concentrated in the bigger forms at the top of the food chain. These nutrients are then broken down, moving from the big creatures to the smaller ones and on to the fungi, bacteria, and other microbes underground. The organic riches the invisible throngs fabricate are taken from there back above the surface in growing plants, then moved into the plant-eaters and their microbiomes, the predators and their microbiomes. Then they are broken down again in the big animals' dung and in the bodies that eventually become food for scavengers and a succession of smaller decomposers and recyclers, whose activities make the nutrients accessible to growing plant roots and mycorrhizae again. Talk about a recycling program!

In many ways, this concentration of species and processes acts like a single great organism. Although that comparison may be stretching the facts, an African savanna definitely does operate as a whole that is greater, more vibrant, and more enduring than the sum of its particular living parts because the whole includes the transfer and release of biotic material and energies constantly going on at all levels between organisms. It's a design for continuous regeneration—or, if you like, continuous reincarnation. Nearly every ecosystem is.

Life in all its invisible and visible designs greatly expands the total surface area of the living planet. Surfaces are where organisms interact with their environment and one another. Yuval Noah Harari points out in his book *Sapiens: A Brief History of*

Humankind that plant leaves alone create three-and-a-half times as much surface area as all the planet's land offers. He goes on to note that if the globe's total surface of land plus its total surface of water is defined as one Earth area, the surfaces of algae in the oceans add three to eight more Earth areas. The surfaces of fungal threads in and on the land add another two to nine Earth areas. Plant root and root-hair surfaces add forty Earth areas, while the surfaces of the bacteria and archaea cells that perfuse the lands and seas from top to bottom contribute 70 to 350 more Earth areas. That many Earth areas worth of surface make the term biosphere a perfect description. Between the uppermost, space-bordering limit of the atmosphere, with its wind-carried spores and bacteria, and layers of rock that rest miles underground yet are still inhabited by microorganisms, this planet is one big rotating stage filled with action at every level.

· · ·

Now that genetic testing is automated and more affordable, sending a DNA sample to a company that will trace your family tree has become very popular. A quick swab of the inside of your cheek or just a little bit of your saliva is all that's required. It often reveals surprising results in terms of people's racial and ethnic backgrounds. The analysis can even tell you whether or not there is a bit of Neanderthal DNA in your lineage. *Homo neanderthalensis* may have diverged from the line that eventually led to *Homo sapiens* as early as 800,000 years ago. *Homo sapiens*, arose in Africa about 450,000 years later. They began expanding north perhaps 250,000 years ago*, and the evidence seems indisputable that some Neanderthals interbred with these most "modern" humans before disappearing around 40,000 years ago.

neanderthalensis
nee-and-er-thal-
en-sis

Yet all that is relatively recent news in the history of species considered human. This category of primate—all members of the genus *Homo*—arose 2.8 million years ago from more ancient hominids nurtured by Africa's woodlands and plains with their wealth of live surfaces and symbioses above and below the surface of the ground.

It seems that anybody curious about the history of his or her ancestors would be interested in a tour of that old family home. How I wish the Ferris wheel I described existed somewhere. Short of that, maybe somebody could create one rotating from the savanna's leafy attic to its busy basement in a virtual reality program. Instead of indirectly piecing together how everything in this ecosystem connects with everything else, we could watch it happening. Cycling round and round on safari between the big beasts that attract our interest and the normally invisible multitudes that power most of the living world, we'd be taking in the full whirl of nature in the place where so much of human nature was forged.

* I cringe a little each time I give an estimated earliest date or location for some major event in the history of humans and their ancestors. Every few years, it seems, a new fossil find causes paleontologists to once again seriously revise the latest picture they had drawn of our past.

NEXT SPREAD

A vulture's-eye view of a great migratory wildebeest herd of the Serengeti moving over a sea of grass like the plasm of a colossal amoeba.
DANIEL ROSENGREN

Rescue at Sea, Part One

In the prologue, I promised to describe examples of conservation programs with a proven record of success at countering the depletion of Earth's pageant of species. The story of the first example starts here.

. . .

I love the wide-open freedom of sailing—the unbounded view in every direction, the feeling of isolation from the rest of the world and its problems, keeping company with the wind and sun and stars instead. Looking up from the deck to see the top of oncoming waves while a gale moans in the rigging? Not so much. But you don't get one without the other in the Atlantic a couple hundred miles off Nova Scotia. I was traveling in the summer with a crew trying to learn more about some highly

evolved fellow mammals that are rarely seen and little known despite being twenty-five to thirty feet long: northern bottlenose whales. During earlier ventures, the researchers had tried a sort of mad scientist take on early harpooning, chasing these creatures through the waves in hopes of jabbing them with a long pole tipped with a big breakaway suction cup attached to a time-depth recorder, locator beacon, and small float. But the team could ... never ... get ... quite ... close enough to a whale before

A typically small group of northern bottlenose whales off Nova Scotia. They belong to a large but poorly known toothed whale family of extreme deep divers, the Ziphiidae. FLIP NICKLIN/MINDEN PICTURES

it sounded. So, they brought a crossbow for this voyage and fitted the suction cup and accompanying gizmos to the end of an arrow.

We sailed 1,600 miles during the trip, most of them while crisscrossing the surface of a deep-sea trench called the Gully looking for bottlenoses to shoot at with the world's clunkiest projectile. Between the rolling Atlantic, moving whales, and arrows that soared with all the grace of a flung toilet plunger—if they ever did strike their target, they hit at the wrong angle for the suction cup to stick—every shot was a bust. *Almost* every shot. Near the expedition's end, one arrow flew straight and true. The cup stuck, and the recording device disappeared with the whale into the deep. Twenty-eight hours later, the suction cup worked loose, and the float carried it and the instrument package to the surface. We set a course for the beacon's signal and dip-netted the gear out of the sea, hooting and fist-pumping like starving castaways who had finally nabbed a fish to eat.

After downloading the time-depth data, Sascha Hooker, the ship's captain and lead scientist, announced with another hoot that this mammal had been making descents of half a mile to nearly a full mile into the abyss beneath us. Using the organic version of a sonar (echolocation) system built into its big domed head, the whale was hunting squid down there in the cold and utter darkness, where the water pressure builds to a ton per square inch—and doing it for as long as seventy minutes at a stretch. How a warm-blooded air-breather can pull off a feat like that is almost impossible to imagine. I can't hold my breath for much more than a minute and a half. Expert freedivers can do it for about ten minutes. As it turns out, the bottlenose whales don't even have to try. The pressure in the abyss squeezes their lungs nearly flat, and they rely on high concentrations of the protein molecule myoglobin in their blood to store extra oxygen and supply it to the muscles.

Like everyone aboard, I put in shifts at the helm and up in the crow's nest to scan the rolling horizon for telltale spouts from a blowhole. For a while, though, I was spending every spare minute down in the hold searching instead for live insects or spiders in the crannies to feed an exhausted warbler that had taken refuge on the ship's deck. But the bird was too drained. It barely responded to the food. After a while, it expired where it had landed, changing from an animal as warm-blooded as any whale to a cold little puff of feathers stirred only by the winds. Had it perked up and taken to the air again, its sole chance for finding solid ground in this blue stretch of the planet would have been Sable Island, about fifty miles away. Even then, the warbler might not have survived on the isle's storm-swept marshes and sand dune grasslands for long. But there's always the chance that it could have. Always a chance.

· · ·

Oceanic islands are, by definition, disconnected chunks of dry ground marooned amid saltwater. Seabirds are able to reach most of them, and they use many as predator-free rookeries for part of the year. An island's mix of other life forms is more random. It is created by the lucky descendants of seeds washed ashore after a long salty voyage or transported stuck to a seabird's feet or feathers, and from four-legged animals that arrived clinging to a log or a mass of floating debris. The community may also include land-dwelling birds that ventured out from another island or nearby mainland, or, like the warbler, got

The last known thylacine, a large, striped marsupial carnivore better known as the Tasmanian tiger (or Tasmanian wolf), died in the Hobart Zoo, Tasmania, in 1936, her species driven to extinction in the wild by European settlers with guns and poisons. JOHN CARNEMOLLA/ GETTY IMAGES

caught aloft in a storm and blown off course, and found itself lost out over the unforgiving sea.

On average, the farther offshore an island is, the lower the number of different species that have been able to reach that ground and go on to successfully colonize it. That's rule number one of island biogeography. Rule number two is that the variety of species—biodiversity—is highest on big islands and lowest on the littlest islands. This is because smaller islands don't have the room to support high populations, and small populations with a restricted range are less able to cope with the challenges fate brings their way. On the mainland, a population knocked dangerously low by storms, wildfires, an epidemic, or other environmental stressor might have its numbers and gene pool refreshed by wanderers from adjoining areas. Stranded on an isle, a population is entirely on its own, and the smaller it is, the more vulnerable it becomes to extinction.

Not many arrivals are likely to survive long in an unfamiliar island environment. But if their luck holds and they find ways to adjust, they'll reproduce and become better and better adapted through generations of natural selection. In time, this may transform the colonists into different species. As a result, even though islands generally have a more limited array of organisms than mainlands, they tend to end up with a higher percentage of endemic species—life forms unique to a particular locale.

Some islands created long ago are like time capsules, preserving flora and fauna from an earlier geologic age. For instance, the evergreen plants known as cycads, commonplace in the Jurassic days when brontosaurs walked the continents, remain a prominent form of vegetation in isolated New Guinea. The thylacine, popularly called the Tasmanian tiger or Tasmanian wolf, was the largest marsupial carnivore left in the modern era. Though present in Australia, it went extinct there, probably under pressure from Aboriginal colonists and competition from feral populations of their dogs—dingoes. Yet thylacines continued to flourish some 150 miles away on the island of Tasmania until the nineteenth century, when a government-sponsored bounty on their striped and toothy heads ramped up persecution by European settlers. Earth's last known living thylacine died in captivity in 1936. The smaller carnivores known as Tasmanian devils continue to survive on the island, though they were declared endangered in 2008. Interestingly, enough people continue to report the odd thylacine sighting in the forests of far northern Queensland, Australia, that scientists have set up remote cameras to check on the slight possibility that a few persist there. Always a chance.

thylacine
thy-luh-sain

The absence of any big predators mostly explains the evolution of endemic flightless birds on a number of islands—a cormorant in the Galápagos, an ibis in Jamaica, New Zealand's namesake kiwi, and its kakapo, or owl parrot, to name just a few. Similarly, an absence of large native herbivores helps explain the presence of endemic island plants lacking the spines or bitter chemicals their nearest mainland relatives defend themselves with. And the absence of either large grazers or close plant competitors may be one of the reasons some ordinarily small forms of vegetation have evolved into unique shrub-size or even tree-size species on islands.

Giantism occurs with certain island animals as well. The elephant bird of Madagascar stood almost ten feet tall, and the giant moa of New Zealand reached nearly twelve feet with its head upraised. Both went extinct following the arrival of humans. The endangered San Esteban Island chuckwalla and threatened Angel Island chuckwalla in the Gulf of California are two to three times the size of their counterparts on the mainland. Although the Komodo dragons on Indonesian islands may be another example of island giantism—some reach lengths of ten feet—they could also represent the time-capsule effect, being holdovers from an earlier period when hulking members of this reptile family, the monitor lizards, were more widespread.

On other islands, isolation and inbreeding within small populations appear to have taken the opposite course, leading to dwarfism. Mammoths no larger than ponies inhabited the Channel Islands off California, and fossils of diminutive elephants have been found on islands in the Mediterranean and parts of the Indonesian archipelago. Their normal-size ancestors

Almost twelve feet tall with its neck upstretched, the flightless moa, New Zealand's largest native animal, disappeared after the arrival of the Maori people. Here, two tourists photograph a re-creation of a moa at Arthur's Pass, New Zealand, 1995. HARUHIKO SAMESHIMA

must have reached those areas during phases of the Ice Ages when so much of the planet's water was locked up in massive glaciers that sea levels fell, leaving many islands connected by land bridges to the continents or else no more than a short swim away. Once rising seas restricted the islands' four-legged inhabitants to a finite territory, giant mammals with giant appetites would have been increasingly hard-pressed to find enough forage. Individuals with smaller bodies must have enjoyed enough

*Found on several
Indonesian islands,
Komodo dragons are
the largest surviving
members of the moni-
tor lizard family. They
scavenge carcasses
and hunt prey such as
Timor rusa deer and
the occasional unwary
feral goat.* MI. SHA/
GETTY IMAGES

floresiensis
floor-s-ian-sis

Denisovans
Den-i-sov-ins

of an advantage that natural selection continued shrinking such species to match the resources available.

Three more curiosities from the island worlds of minipachyderms: First, on the Indonesian island of Flores, where a pygmy version of an elephant once dwelled, fossils discovered in 2003 suggest that early humans living there may have undergone downsizing as well. Judging from remains found so far, the tallest of those folks stood just a smidgen over three-and-a-half feet high. Dubbed *Homo floresiensis* by paleontologists and Hobbits by the media, they existed until perhaps 50,000 or 60,000 years ago, making them contemporaries of *Homo sapiens*, Neanderthals, and the recently discovered Denisovans of

Asia. Second, the Cyclops of Homer's Odyssey who captured Odysseus (Ulysses) and his crew of mariners on an isle in the Aegean Sea was likely based on legends that arose after people on Mediterranean islands uncovered strange skulls with what looked like the socket for a single large eye in the center of the facial bones. In reality, it was the nasal passageway for the trunk of an undersized elephant. Lastly, smaller-than-normal woolly mammoths survived on Wrangel Island in the Arctic Ocean north of Siberia until between 2500 and 2000 BC. Although they had been in decline due to inbreeding, the last disappeared about the time human hunters finally reached that remote spot. How wondrous would it be if they had left a few?

. . .

Nobody can provide the exact number of islands the world's oceans hold since there is no "official" standard for the size that a coral reef, sandy shoal, or exposed rock ledge has to be to qualify as an island. Geographers' best guess is that there are about 465,000 oceanic islands. Collectively, they account for a bit less than 5.5 percent of Earth's total land area. Yet more than 60 percent of the known extinctions on Earth since 1500 AD have taken place on them. And nearly all of those were caused by late-arriving species, the foremost among them being us. We kept coming in vessels small and large seeking fresh water and food or a safe haven to wait out a storm or make repairs. More voyagers showed up looking for trade routes, treasure, marine mammal pelts, or to claim new domain for a ruler or to establish a fishing or whaling station. As navigation and shipbuilding technologies improved, fewer and fewer of even the most remote islands went unvisited.

Once there, folks did what they were used to doing every-where else. They hunted, trapped, fished, collected eggs, and, where possible, settled, cleared forests, and planted crops. For vulnerable island species, many of which had been without pred-ators or other enemies so long that they had no natural defenses, the consequences of human foraging, habitat disturbance, and commercial harvest of wildlife were dire. Where the mariners led pigs, goats, sheep, rabbits, chickens, other livestock, or dogs down the gangplank, or the ship's cats found a way to shore on their own, the negative effects were further magnified. And inad-vertently, the seafarers also introduced three stowaways: brown rats (Norway rats), black rats, and the house mouse, all of which have excelled for millennia at keeping people and their food supplies company wherever they go.

How many islands do you think suddenly got colonized by rats and mice from boats that never even touched the shore? Picture those animals scurrying among provisions deep in the hold, where leaking water would first begin to collect in a ves-sel run afoul of a shoal or reef. Now envision the panicked peo-ple aboard suddenly realizing just how many rodents had been living below as the animals came swarming up onto the decks; yes, the proverbial rats fleeing a sinking ship. Prolific breeders and indiscriminate omnivores, able to make meals of vegeta-bles, grains, fruits, fungi, insects, crustaceans, eggs, just about any live vertebrate they can catch, and the carcasses of those that died from various causes, rats generally had the best odds of any animal associated with humans for surviving where a boat wrecked or made landfall.

Cats are more strictly carnivorous than rats but also very adaptable. When other food is scarce, they can get by scrounging for insects, other invertebrates such as crustaceans and mollusks in the tidal zone, and remains of fish and other marine life washed up on the beaches. Like rats, cats are also agile climbers, able to reach seabirds nesting in trees and on the steep, rocky slopes of pinnacle rookeries. Some of the common house mice that reached islands developed the habit of eating seabird hatchlings alive and gnawing even older juveniles to death as the still-flightless young wait for their parents to return to feed them. But the rats stand out as the most pervasive scourge of seabirds, devouring adults, young, and eggs alike in crowded nesting sites. Their plundering has been responsible for much of the massive decline of seabirds worldwide as well as for a majority of the known island extinctions of other birds, reptiles, and mammals, and the sharp reduction or disappearance of many island plants.

Besides the words invasive and introduced, biologists often use the term non-native to describe species that arrive in unfamiliar areas and find ways to flourish there, very often at the expense of some resident forms of life. These are confusing labels when applied to the later inhabitants of oceanic islands because so many of the earlier ones also got there by happenstance, making them non-native invaders themselves. The difference is that most island species got there long ago and had time to establish some sort of balance within the ecosystem—an equilibrium disrupted by more modern arrivals, most notably *Homo sapiens.*

Stated that way, the last sentence sounds a little like a rebuke, as though I'm assigning guilt. I'm not. In fact, I think we environmental writers might want to reconsider our habit of shaming humans for having acted like humans. I could just as truly write that our species has a special gift for dreaming about what's over the edge of the known world, trying out new things, successfully adapting to different circumstances, and going on from there. Exploration has always been part of our inventiveness, taking humanity to settings never before imagined.

As we introduced ourselves to island after island, they introduced us to all manner of strange and wondrous creatures. Throughout the time of island colonization by early seafaring cultures and later exploration driven by national and commercial interests, few, if any, who stepped ashore were worrying about the impacts their activities would have on local life forms. The world still seemed a huge, mysterious place, its oddities and marvels countless and its bounties nigh-inexhaustible.

Reaching land—any land—in a big raft, outrigger canoe, or other early craft after weeks or months on the open ocean; *that* was a worry. Prior to the late eighteenth century, scurvy was still regularly claiming the lives of as many as half of naval crews on long voyages; that was a worry. Neither the cause of this ailment (lack of vitamin C in the diet) nor the reasons that infectious diseases spread by sailors all but wiped out native people on some islands were understood. Nobody paused to fret about some rats scampering away from supplies piled on shore or about the fact that a couple of shipboard cats went missing. Nobody cautioned that the goats let loose on an island to ensure a ready supply of fresh meat for the next visit might munch tasty native plants clean out of existence and disrupt habitats that endemic animals depended upon to survive. While some island-bound cultures understood the concept of natural balance, the terms "ecology" and "wildlife conservation" wouldn't be part of *Homo sapiens'* common vocabulary until the twentieth century.

The true number of species that went extinct on the globe since the arbitrary date of 1500 CE (common era) is unknown because neither science, such as it was, nor local cultures kept track of many types of creatures that vanished. Depending on how historical records are interpreted, the minimum count of (mainly vertebrate) life forms experts think went extinct after that date is usually put between about 750 and 1,000. Not only did a majority of those extinctions take place on islands, invasive animals—most of them introduced by humans—played a role in 86 percent of the disappearances.

Today, tens of thousands of species around the world are on lists that variously designate them as at risk, rare, very rare, or threatened with extinction. The species closest to the brink of oblivion are designated endangered or critically endangered. Those two categories now contain 2,919 species of terrestrial vertebrates. And 1,189 of them—319 amphibians, 282 reptiles, 296 birds, and 292 mammals—are on islands.

If this is to be one of the chapters that highlight examples of how to go about saving nature right now—and avoid scolding people for their peopleness—why, then, am I pointing out yet another muddle humanity has made of living systems it encountered? Because there is a clear way to get through this time-crunch for island species and come out feeling a lot better about their future and ourselves by proving that we really can save a whole lot in a hurry.

NEXT SPREAD

Eye to eye with a curious forty-five-foot-long sea monster. After spending the summer in arctic waters, the main population of gray whales returns south to shallow lagoons along Mexico's Baja Peninsula, a round trip of 10,000 to 14,000 miles.
FLORIAN SCHULZ

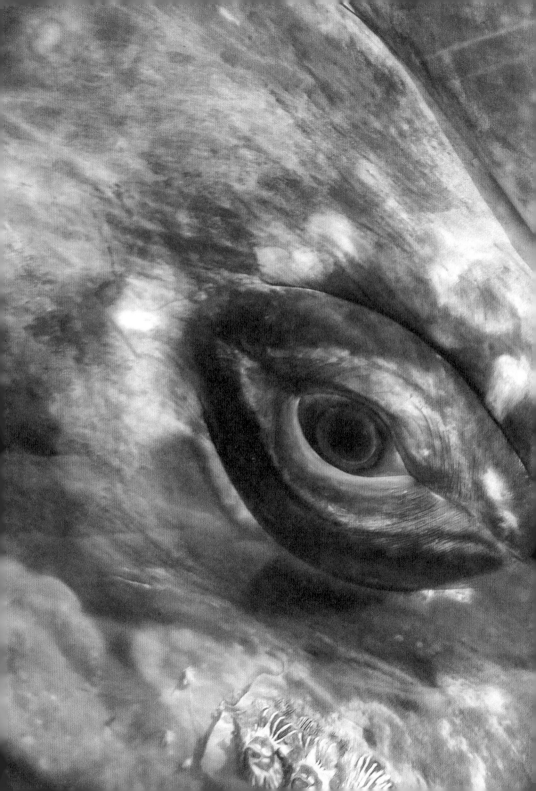

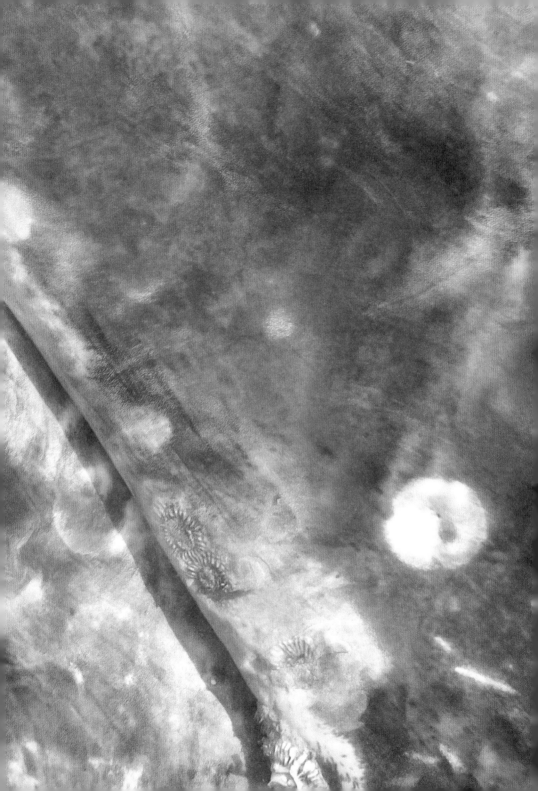

CHAPTER NINE

Rescue at Sea, Part Two

Reaching lengths of nearly 100 feet and weighing up to 190 tons, the blue whale is the largest animal Earth has produced—ever. Perhaps the most important statistics are counts showing populations rebounding from near-extinction caused by commercial whaling. NOAA

One day in the waters around the Channel Islands off California, a curious whale approached and surfaced next to the skiff I was in. The visitor's sleek topside stretched for forty feet in front of the craft and for another forty behind, and its breath shot water vapor thirty feet into the sky. This was a blue whale—hundred-ton body, heart the size of a smart car, tongue that matches the weight of an elephant, and all the other superlatives that go with being the biggest breed of animal nature ever concocted. To have one visit so close that I could have reached out and touched it felt like an honor.

That blue whale encounter came during a period a couple decades ago when I was getting out of bed most mornings to go look for this species somewhere in the North Pacific. My companions for most of the time that I spent among the Channel

Islands' blues were two professors I had never observed at sea, around town, or inside an academic office wearing anything but faded shorts and T-shirts. In an earlier book, *The Grandest of Lives: Eye to Eye with Whales*, I wrote:

> *I rode along on an old fishing boat retrofitted for science by Don Croll and Bernie Tershy of the University of California, Santa Cruz. To say the craft*

had a lived-in feel would be generous. The cramped wheelhouse was a jumble of instrument wires, student assistants, drying clothing, and notebooks next to the remains of dinner from the night before—or possibly a couple of nights before—and laptop computers whose monitors danced with colors highlighting the krill swarms detected by instruments scanning the depths with sound. In its anarchic way, everything was prepped for gathering crucial data. When wind and chop and fog prevented that, what did the scientists do? Dude, they went surfing. This was California, after all. Locating a point off a lonely island where the swell made totally excellent waves, Croll and Tershy unlashed their boards from the boat's roof and passed the day on the breakers' slopes, kicking out from the curl at the last moment before their ride slammed into the ragged volcanic rock on shore. We camped on the island at night, laying out sleeping bags on the sand beneath the stars.

Croll, Tershy, and I were shipmates again in the island-stippled Gulf of California between the Baja Peninsula and Mexico's mainland. During that trip, we had blue whales plus the second-largest animals on earth, fin whales, in view. Both were skim-feeding at times, swallowing swarms of krill along the surface. But they were more often diving about 500 feet down into the ocean trench running north-south along the center of the Gulf, where they could gulp still denser concentrations of krill. An extension of the San Andreas Fault, this trench is almost two miles deep in places. Nutrient-rich water upwelling from its depths fuels one of the

simplest, straightest, most productive food chains in nature: prodigious blooms of single-celled algae feed masses of half-inch-
long krill feed gargantuan whales.

For Croll, understanding these whales meant looking at how
changing ocean conditions influenced the ecology of krill. Yet
as we cruised close to a cliffside where cacti rose wreathed with
vines, I learned that his expertise extended above the waves too.
With a majority of nations observing a moratorium on hunting
whales, he told me, most of the animals were now less imperiled
than many of the plants, birds, reptiles, and mice on the islands
around us. Mice? Yes, native species and subspecies of them
endemic to particular islands. Like other plants and animals,
they were succumbing to cats and introduced rodents.

While plenty of people were enthusiastic supporters of
protecting whales, Croll noted, few were paying attention to
the smaller and, in many cases, one-of-a-kind creatures on the
isles the giants swam past. As he spoke, I remembered a Baja
fisherman taking me, a friend, and two kayaks about forty miles
out into the Sea of Cortez to leave us as the only humans on
Isla Catalina (or Catalina Island, to distinguish it from Santa
Catalina Island off California's coast). We camped there for several weeks and paddled, snorkeled among sea lions, and lived on
the fish we caught and the bag of dried corn flour we made into
tortillas. A strikingly large species of barrel cactus found only on
several Gulf islands grew from the slopes along with giant cardon, the world's tallest cactus (which owes much of its growth on
this stony, thirsty, sun-cooked ground to a combination of symbiotic mycorrhizae and nitrogen-fixing bacteria). While wander-
ing among the spiky vegetation, I also encountered a couple of
the local rattlesnakes—quiet types; they had no noise-making

The world's tallest cactus, the giant cardon, grows in Sonora and Baja, Mexico, on poor soils under extremely dry conditions with the help of symbiotic mycorrhizae and nitrogen-fixing bacteria surrounding its roots. LÉON DIGUET

segments at the end of their tail. One of seven reptile species unique to Isla Catalina, the rattle-less rattlesnake probably became that way because the isolated population evolved for millennia with no predatory mammals to warn off.

Almost 50 of the 115 reptile species inhabiting the islands in the Gulf of California exist nowhere else. Because so many unique types arose over time as their mainland ancestors adapted to the particular conditions of various islands, this archipelago makes a natural laboratory for the study of evolution. It's a sort of Galápagos North where the ability of organisms to fine-tune their form and function to fit slight variations in the environment is on clear display. During the course of their marine studies, Croll and Tershy kept close track of the flora and fauna on these islands and in 1997 went on to set up a nonprofit organization with the purpose of protecting those species. They named the group Island Conservation.

With assistance from the Mexican government and local volunteers, Island Conservation's small staff started working to remove rodents and cats—and occasionally feral goats, dogs, or other introduced animals—from islands throughout the Gulf of California region. There is no way to romanticize this side of the wildlife-saving business. More often than not, it involved trudging across the terrain to lace it with traps and poisoned baits. Volunteers on foot could systematically cover the entirety of a small island without too much trouble, but an eradication program for a larger island might require broadcasting the baits from an aircraft and doing it more than once. In other cases, native inhabitants like the endemic mice, which might eat the bait themselves, had to be captured and removed to a holding area, then reintroduced after weathering broke down the rodenticides scattered about.

Conditions such as treacherous seacliff terrain posed additional challenges. Even so, the programs still proved cheaper and easier to accomplish than many other kinds of conservation work, especially since most of the islands in the Gulf of California are too small, rocky, and parched to support permanent human habitation. Compared with trying to stave off extinction for black rhinos in ever-more populated southern Africa, piping plovers along the ever-busier Atlantic seaboard of North America, or the few hundred Siberian tigers remaining in Russia's Far East amid ever-expanding road systems for logging operations, killing rats that have taken over an island with few or no people begins to look like a pass through the garden pulling weeds.

I don't mean the last sentence to sound too indifferent to the fate of the invasive animals. One afternoon on Isla San Pedro Mártir near the center of the Gulf, I returned from a snorkel foray to talk with biologist Araceli Samaniego on the beach. We had been visiting a number of islands in the area. At each one, she set

... rescuing a bit more than 40 percent of the terrestrial vertebrates closest to vanishing from the planet forever [is] doable, not just within our lifetimes but much sooner ...

out live traps to sample the terrain for invasive rodents. Working for the Mexican nonprofit Grupo de Ecologia y Conservación de Islas, she was particularly concerned about a sharp decline in the breeding colony of red-tailed tropicbirds on San Pedro Mártir.

When we rendezvoused, she had just climbed down from the cliff face where she was checking a nesting site. Wordlessly, she thrust her hand my direction. It was filled with gnawed infant tropicbird bones. Samaniego began to shake her head slowly. Finally, she muttered, "Rats. Everywhere." When she found one in the next trap that she checked, she took the rodent's measurements. Then she put it to death. This was the same genial, soft-spoken woman I'd watched coo at the small endemic mice caught in her live traps, gently taking them out to stroke their delicate feet and talk to them, calling them sweetheart—*corazón*—before she turned them loose. She wasn't comfortable executing rats; in fact, she looked miserable. Yet she eliminated every one she caught.

For anyone who values all life, the extermination of invasive animals that have been exterminating resident species is not a clear-cut choice between right and wrong. It is a judgment call in

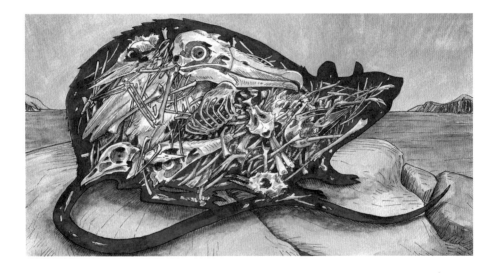

favor of the natural diversity of life—saving imperiled creatures at the expense of creatures whose kind will very likely remain superabundant elsewhere on the globe.

While it may be hard to carry out such a purge without twinges of conflicting emotions, there is nothing ambivalent about the results. Take away feral goats, and plants that hadn't been seen for years and were feared extinct pop up through the ground from long-dormant seeds. Take out introduced predators, and before long nearly vanished lizards become regularly sighted

Common stowaways in the larders of ships, rats that reached oceanic islands with few or no natural predators have been responsible for the majority of extinctions of native animals and the collapse of seabird nesting colonies.
SARAH GILMAN

and rare, ground-nesting resident songbirds reappear. Especially satisfying for Croll, Tershy, and colleagues like Samaniego, who share a special interest in seabirds, what had become shrunken or completely abandoned rookeries began to fill the air around islands once again with their cries and clouds of wings.

Look at that! Done! Next?

. . .

More people looked and saw a model worth building on. The programs for eradicating invasives were proving spectacularly effective on island after island. Equally rewarding, the results showed up almost immediately. As the early successes of Island Conservation resulted in more private donations and institutional grants, answers to the question, Where next? began to include South Pacific atolls and islands off Australia and South America. As Island Conservation grew, it took on projects together with Birdlife International, The Nature Conservancy, the International Union for Conservation of Nature (IUCN), and other partners including a variety of universities and national governments.

How many people care about a rattle-less rattlesnake? Who even knew there is such a thing as a Ricords iguana on Isla Cabritos in the Dominican Republic, much less that it is critically endangered? How many had ever heard about the critically endangered *tutururu*, or Polynesian ground dove, originally present on a number of South Pacific isles including Tahiti and Moorea but reduced by rat and cat depredation to fewer than 200 birds spread across five atolls in French Polynesia? Who knew that on some islands, you needed to fling poisoned bait up into the trees of every grove to be sure they reached the rats living off nesting birds in the branches? As it turned out, enough people knew and cared and combined their efforts that more island projects got underway every year.

To date, Island Conservation has led or helped with successful projects completed on at least sixty-four islands, including the largest yet—1,450-square-mile South Georgia Island in the subantarctic region of the southern Atlantic. There, it took several years and three island-wide dispersals of bait from helicopters for a team overseen by Anthony Martin of the University of Dundee to successfully eradicate the rats that had devastated breeding colonies of seabirds—among them, albatrosses, penguins, and a cormorant unique to South Georgia. The rats were eating their way through an endemic species of pipit (a type of songbird) and endemic pintail ducks as well. With its partners, Island Conservation can now claim to have restored about 1,200 populations of 490 species and subspecies worldwide.

Not long ago, Island Conservation and the Coastal and Conservation Action Laboratory of the University of California, Santa Cruz, formed a plan with experts from Birdlife International and the Invasive Species Specialist Group of the IUCN. The scientists combed through all the available information about the distribution of highly threatened island vertebrates and of invasive vertebrates, interviewed more than 500 other authorities on the subject, and created a worldwide Threatened Island Biodiversity Database. With this overview, they can now precisely answer the question of where the next eradication programs should be focused to do the most good for the most species of native, island-dwelling animals.

A 2017 paper titled "Globally Threatened Vertebrates on Islands with Invasive Species," published in *Science Advances*, put the value of this approach to protecting nature in perspective.

Its lead author was Island Conservation biologist Dena Spatz. Not surprisingly, Croll and Tershy were among the coauthors. The article began by pointing out that while the 1,189 highly imperiled species of vertebrates on islands add up to only 5 percent of Earth's terrestrial vertebrate species, they make up a little over 40 percent of all those considered endangered or critically endangered. These imperiled animals have breeding populations on 1,288 islands, barely 1/4 of 1 percent of the world's islands. Is this beginning to sound like a problem on a scale modern civilization could handle if more people turned their attention to it?

Reliable information on the presence or absence of introduced vertebrates was only available for 1,030 of those islands. It turns out that 247 of them don't have such invaders. Therefore, the paper concludes, if we can control or eliminate the invasive vertebrates known to be on the remaining 783 islands, it could lead to the recovery of close to four of every ten of the planet's terrestrial vertebrate species on the verge of extinction. There you go. This is how you save a big slice of the planet's biological diversity as quickly as possible—and do it for a whole lot less money and effort than it would take to save 40 percent of the endangered and critically endangered vertebrate species on the rest of Earth's land surface.

Seeing natural shrubs and trees regrow on an island because invaders are no longer eating most of the seeds or sprouts isn't just rewarding for botanists concerned about rare plants. The recovery of that vegetation stabilizes and enriches the soil, encouraging the growth of more plants that various native animal inhabitants depend on. Before rats were eliminated on Palmyra Atoll, a lonely wisp of emergent coral reef between the

Hawaiian Islands and American Samoa, researchers counted the
seedlings of five native tree species including the tall *Pisonia
grandis*, a key nesting habitat for seabirds. The total was 150 new
sprouts. Five years after the removal of rats, the tally was 7,700
sprouts. The survey team also noticed two species of land crabs
that had never been seen on the atoll when rats were abundant.

Pisonia grandis
Piso-ni-a gran-dis

Knowing that a seabird colony on a tropical isle is flourishing again is a soaring delight in itself. Knowing that as the nutrients from the guano deposits in and around healthy rookeries
wash back into the ocean they improve the health and diversity of life tied to coral reefs in the area magnifies that feeling.
Investigators recently reported that the reefs around tropical
islands without rats were definitely growing faster, putting the
corals in a stronger position to cope with the stress of warming
oceans and rising sea levels. Moreover, the biomass of reef fish
was half again as large as it was around isles where the rodents
reigned on shore. Islands may be disconnected from mainlands,

but they are as connected as can be within their own landscape's ecosystem and with the surrounding sea. And they will always be among the wildest, most remote, and most enchanting settings on Earth.

The island biodiversity database notes that humans are absent or have only a minimal presence on a majority of the islands with highly at-risk vertebrates. That makes rescuing a bit more than 40 percent of the terrestrial vertebrates closest to vanishing from the planet forever all the more doable, not just within our lifetimes but much sooner if enough people jump on board and help.

Look at that! All done! Next?

Ode to a Strawberry

Amid the heap of Rocky Mountains in Montana's Glacier National Park is a summit 7,200 feet high. It's a knoll compared to the 9,000-foot-plus crags in the neighborhood and barely nudges above tree line. But this lower peak has glories of its own. After a wildfire burned the forest on its south side years ago, the seared ground healed over into meadows where butterflies gather to sip nectars while pollinating fireweed blossoms, rosy pussytoes, dwarf forget-me-nots, harebells, lupines, sulfur flowers—and the small, white, ground-hugging blossoms that turn into strawberries.

When a long climb leads you to ripe wild strawberries shouting in scarlet about how they want to be put inside somebody's mouth, you oblige. And the chances that you'll remember ever eating anything better start fading fast. You're busy chewing, nodding, sighing, looking for more strawberries, and not thinking about much of anything for the moment.

Later, you might come out of your strawberry stupor wondering what makes this fruit taste that good. It turns out to be a loaded question that gets at the nature of nature as well as anything. Instead of having to roam a whole ecosystem, like a savanna, to put together the picture of how life works, you can find the same principles converging in a single fruit that fits splendidly in your mouth.

Like most juicy packets containing plant offspring, strawberries are designed to encourage animals to eat them. In this setting, the berries successfully bribe ground squirrels, least chipmunks, spruce grouse, jays, ravens, mule deer, snowshoe hares, ambling bears—and passing hikers—to dine on them and spread the seeds around in the animal's droppings. Do strawberries need to be this scrumptious to accomplish that? It seems that if they were only two-thirds or just half as yummy, you'd still

There are more than a hundred natural species and subspecies of strawberry—and at least 600 varieties now developed through cultivation. This nineteenth-century engraving highlights varieties of the Eurasian strawberry Fragaria vesca. ÉDOUARD MAUBERT/ALAMY PHOTO

go after them, and the animals would too. But would they do it quite as often or for quite as long before turning to other fare? It tastes as though strawberries have opted not to take that risk.

There have to be sound biological reasons linked to survival for a plant to concoct such flamboyantly flavorful fruit. Either that, or strawberries are evidence that the universe, for all its random hazards and impenetrable mysteries, is up to something wonderful. Or maybe those are just two different ways of talking about the phenomenon of life on Earth that ultimately say the same thing.

. . .

Familiar and well-liked, strawberries are part of the rose family. They make up the genus *Fragaria* with more than twenty species growing in different temperate regions of the globe. Early humans surely snacked on them during their migration from Africa into Eurasia. At late Stone Age sites, archeologists have found evidence that people were gathering the fruits for meals at home. With the rise of kingdoms and empires, the fruits or their seeds were being traded throughout the Middle East, along the Great Silk Road, and in parts of South America.

Although the wood strawberry of Eurasia had been cultivated in early Persia for centuries, the practice apparently didn't become popular in Western Europe until late medieval times. In the 1750s, growers in France crossed the hardy Virginia strawberry, found wild over much of North America, with the beach strawberry, a native of the Pacific Coast from Alaska to Chile that produces larger-than-average fruits. The result was an extra-plump and delicious, yet reliably sturdy new kind of strawberry in the world. Its common name is the garden strawberry, because this hybrid soon became the choice for both home growing and larger-scale agricultural production. It still is.

The purpose of humankind is probably not to help strawberry plants take over the world; things just look that way at times from the middle of furrowed farmland. Although we do toil to ensure that strawberries multiply and gain ground, the benefits flowing back to us reach well beyond satisfying our appetite. Chinese records from 2600 BCE refer to the strawberry as a cleanser of toxins in the body. Native Americans valued the plant for the same reason and for assisting fertility in women. In the Roman empire, *fragum*—the strawberry—was used to treat not only digestive upsets but also depression. It was prescribed as an antidepressant in other cultures as well and remained a traditional remedy for colds, aches, and other common ailments into the modern era.

The wood strawberry was named *Fragaria vesca* by the eighteenth-century Swedish physician, zoologist, and botanist Carl Linnaeus, the same fellow who coined the title of *Homo sapiens* for humankind. During his day, the various schemes biologists used for classifying organisms were proving too arbitrary and unwieldy to cope with the wave of new specimens being collected by naturalist-explorers. Linnaeus devised the now-standardized method for identifying every creature by two Latin labels—the first for genus, followed by a second for species. He assigned names to something like 10,000 kinds of flora and fauna and then grouped related types into broader categories. His taxonomic system cured the growing confusion. The man himself suffered at times from gout, but he had a cure for that as well. Whenever he experienced an attack, Linnaeus ate bowls of strawberries every day, and, he claimed, the flare-up would subside.

Rather than debunk old accounts of strawberry's contributions to wellness, current research tends to validate them. For example, investigators at the Harvard School of Public Health found significantly lower levels of joint inflammation among women eating sixteen or more strawberries a day. Another Harvard study concluded that eating strawberries and blueberries three times a week reduced the chance of a heart attack by 34 percent in women. But given the array of minerals and organic compounds in a strawberry, sorting out which healthful effect is due to a particular ingredient rather than to a combination of factors can turn into a marathon task.

To begin with, a strawberry is rich in vitamin C. One cup (about twelve medium-size berries) supplies the adult daily requirement for this essential nutrient, credited with boosting the immune system and shortening the duration of colds. Vitamin C is a powerful antioxidant, scavenging free radicals that can trigger inflammations and damage tissues. Also known as ascorbic acid, it has a role in preventing hypertension, dilating blood vessels, and counteracting harmful cholesterol. All of these help prevent cardiovascular disease and reduce the possibility of a heart attack or stroke.

The more closely you examine the chemical contents, the more it begins to look as though every wild strawberry amounts to a dose of good medicine. PICTURE PARTNERS/ALAMY PHOTO

Strawberries also come packed with flavonoids which include the red, blue, and purple anthocyanin pigments of plants. These have strong antioxidative qualities and may offer protections against inflammation and cardiovascular disease similar to those gained from vitamin C. Strawberry plants also produce carotenoid pigments, which range from yellow through orange to red. They include lutein and zeaxanthins with antioxidant properties of their own. Another antioxidant from the *Fragaria* pharmacy is the beta-carotene form of vitamin A, which gets reprocessed into compounds that appear to support the immune system and healthy vision. Strawberries don't contain a lot of this stuff, but that doesn't mean you wouldn't gain some of the beneficial effects if you eat enough of these fruits. How many? The jury is still out.

anthocyanin
an-thow-sy-uh-nin

zeaxanthins
zee-uh-zan-thins

The most abundant protein in animals' bodies is collagen. It gives us shape and holds us together by building and repairing bone, cartilage, ligaments, skin, and other connective tissues. The old practice of prescribing strawberries to treat slow-healing wounds (a common symptom of scurvy) is demystified once you know that vitamin C is vital to the making of collagen. Pelargonidin, one of the plant's red pigments, may help protect the skin from ultraviolet radiation in the UVA spectrum. Ellagic acid, a potent antioxidant concentrated in the strawberry's seeds, seems to increase resistance to the sun's higher-energy UVB rays, which can degrade the collagen fibrils of skin tissue and damage the DNA in skin cells.

The interplay of ingredients keeps multiplying as you factor in the berries' supplies of potassium, manganese, calcium, phosphorus, and folates, all critical to keeping a body in good working order. *Fragaria* is by no means uniquely well-endowed with nutrients. Certain fruits and vegetables contain as many or more. So rather than hype the strawberry as a superfood, it is fairer to say it deserves a lofty rank among the plants considered good for you and, compared to most of them, is way more fun to eat.

Nearly 80 percent of the people one researcher interviewed in England said that merely thinking about munching on strawberries made them feel more relaxed and happy and inclined to call up memories of a fair summer day. The Cherokee tribes of the southeastern United States have legends of strawberries mending rifts between people by making them gentler and more kind. Wherever a strawberry slips down somebody's gullet, one of the many things the fruit's vitamin C, potassium, manganese, calcium, and possibly its flavonoids do is promote the production of endorphins. These are natural opioids that function as neurotransmitters. Sometimes called feel-good molecules, they can reduce stress and block the perception of pain. They may also foster a sense of well-being or outright euphoria. This could be partly because one of the effects of endorphins is to stimulate release of another neurotransmitter and psychoactive compound, dopamine, in the brain.

Speaking of feel-goodness, the strawberry has been associated since ancient times with romance. Rouged and succulent, shaped like a swelling heart—an edible valentine, as one writer put it—the fruit was among the symbols of Venus, the Roman goddess of love and fertility, and her Norse counterpart, Freyja. Being one of the first fruits to ripen in spring or early summer, when the world is coming into full flush and marriages begin taking place at the fastest clip of the year, added to the strawberry's reputation as a food of endearment and passion. The French went so far as to feed couples cold strawberry soup on their wedding night.

Now, if *Fragaria* were a full-tilt, jump-start-the-lovin' aphrodisiac, it's almost certain we would all know about that. Still, mix the boundless powers of positive thinking with the fruit's ingredients that improve blood flow, increase vitality in general, and boost endorphin levels, and the combination might lead to ... at the very least a slightly healthier, slightly happier tryst than you'd have had without strawberries. Go on, be a scientist: Experiment!

• • •

Leaving aside the plant's contributions to nutrition and health, the quality that seems most special about a strawberry is its fragrance—the stimulating, sweet-but-not-too-sweet aroma of roses mixed with the singed sugar tones of caramel or maybe pink cotton candy along with a hint of freshly cut grass. Too much?

The Strawberry Thief textile pattern produced by Morris & Co. was inspired by birds that raided these fruits from Mr. Morris's garden. The strawberry has long had roles not only as a cure for ailments and symbol of romance but also as a scrumptious subject for art.
WILLIAM MORRIS

Try a wild strawberry yourself before you answer. The perfume from a platter of berries can fill a room, and the odor from pieces crushed in your mouth largely defines the fruit's taste as the volatile chemicals rise from the throat into the nasal passages.

What is this unmistakable smell made of? To date, laboratory analyses have identified isoamyl hexanoate, 2-methylbutanoic acid, and ... well, another 350 or so barely pronounceable aromatic compounds. Of those, about twenty to thirty are said to be chiefly responsible for the scent people detect. The recipe for assembling and mixing this potion remains *Fragaria's*

isoamyl hexanoate
ahy-soh-am-il hex-a-note

methylbutanoic
meh-thl-beaut-a-no-ic

secret. Strawberry is one of the most popular artificial flavorings worldwide, and makers of candies, perfumes, and cosmetics have come closer to duplicating the fruit's natural flavor over the years. Even so, their best results are still less like the perfect ode to a strawberry than like wannabe poets' rough drafts.

The two molecules thought to be most responsible for the strawberry smell are termed furanoids. These two compounds are not generated by the plant alone. They require the help of bacteria living within strawberry plants' green tissues. The relationship between this microbe, *Methylobacterium extorquens*, and a strawberry is a classic symbiosis, a mutualism that benefits both participants. Colonies of the bacteria gain a favorable environment among the host's cells. They do not feed directly on the tissues but instead absorb and digest methane given off by the plant. In return for its food and lodging, *Methylobacterium* secretes precursor chemicals that spark synthesis of the furanoids. They in turn highlight the strawberry fruit's flavor and fragrance that in turn attracts seed-spreaders.

Rhizophagus irregularis is another symbiotic microbe—a mycorrhizal fungus this time—tied to the strawberry. Binding to the root system, many hundreds of miles of invisibly small *Rhizophagus* threads wind and loop, wander, and poke among the grains of soil, expanding each strawberry plant's ability to acquire moisture and nutrients from the soil far and wide, and deep into crevices too tiny to admit a root. As usual with mycorrhizae, the near end of each fungal thread meanwhile collects a bit of payment for its work directly from the strawberry root's cells, where the currency of sugars and carbohydrates is banked.

The bacterium *Pseudomonas fluorescens* is called a commensal—an organism that regularly lives with another species

furanoid
fur-a-noyd

Methylobacterium extorquens
Meth-ill-o-bak-tear-i-um
x-tor-kens

Rhizophagus irregularis
Ry-zo-fay-gus
ir-reg-u-lar-is

Pseudomonas fluorescens
Soo-duh-mow-nuhs
floor-es-scents

and may contribute to its welfare but does not require anything specific from the host other than tolerance. *Pseudomonas* likes the organic chaff that collects on the surfaces of the strawberry's roots and leaves. The strawberry is the beneficiary of chemicals from *Pseudomonas* that repel or kill harmful bacteria, disease-causing fungi, and some of the microscopic plant-devouring worms known as nematodes. We benefit not only from healthier plants that produce more and better strawberries but also from one of the antibiotics this bacterium manufactures. It's called mupirocin, and it is used to treat skin, ear, and eye infections in humans. Applied to burn victims, it helps counter infection by strains of *Staphylococcus* bacteria resistant to other medicines. It could conceivably save your life one day.

How many organisms altogether go into making a strawberry? Too many to count. *Fragaria* is among the many plants that may form symbiotic relationships with several species of mycorrhizal fungus at a time. Additional fungi and billions of bacteria from a wide spectrum of species are also, like *Pseudomonas*, living on the exterior of nearly every kind of vegetation amid its coating of shed surface cells, waxy or sticky exudates, dust, insects, and bird droppings. Still more microscopic fungi and bacteria live inside most plants' tissues.

Many are temporary visitors or benign hangers-on. Others can be infectious. However, it will come as a surprise if more of the creatures in the micro-menagerie on and around a strawberry aren't found to be assisting the plant in ways besides the most common ones—decomposing stuff, breaking down organic debris, and releasing nutrients that the plant can absorb through its leaves and stems aboveground or through its roots and mycorrhizae. As for the microbes within most plants' tissues, they play so many roles that researchers have long careers ahead of them trying to sort out all the bacteria, archaea, and fungi that may thwart infections from those that may contribute to the manufacture of insect-repelling chemicals, or perform some other helpful function. The more successful investigators are, the farther their discoveries may go toward shifting agricultural production away from a reliance on toxic chemicals and toward less environmentally harmful natural methods to increase crop yields.

Hang in there. You don't get to return to the visible world with a tempting bowl of sliced strawberries on the table just yet. There are two more symbioses between bacteria and strawberry to account for—two ancient, deeply embedded kinds of mutualism that are all-important to plants in general and equally indispensable to us and other animals.

Vegetation relies on photosynthesis, using light from the sun to convert carbon dioxide and water into glucose, a key raw material in the building of more elaborate molecules for growth and reproduction. With apologies for replaying a school biology lesson: cells contain specialized parts known as organelles. Among plants, photosynthesis takes place in the green, chlorophyll-laden organelles called chloroplasts. What you may not have learned in class is that chloroplasts represent an ancient line of bacteria. They were probably cyanobacteria, generally credited with having invented photosynthesis—the biochemical "app" for harnessing solar power—more than 2 billion years ago. Instead of drifting around trying to absorb scattered nutrients from the water they inhabited, these microbes could now tap sunshine to produce their meals internally.

The change made cyanobacteria one of early Earth's predominant life forms. This group of species is still extremely abundant and widespread today. But back when the primordial atmosphere was thick with carbon monoxide, carbon dioxide, and sulfur dioxide, the combined activity of cyanobacteria started the long, planet-altering work of filling the atmosphere with oxygen given off as a byproduct of photosynthesis. Larger single-celled creatures arose, and multitudes of them fed on bacteria. At least one ate a cyanobacterium that must have had an extra-resistant membrane around it or perhaps exuded so many nutrients that the predator never bothered to digest this prey. In any case, the cyanobacterium stayed intact inside, and a symbiosis began. Compared to existence in the open as a wriggling bit of micro-plankton, the bacterium found a more constant and secure habitat inside the host. For its part, the host became less dependent on its success hunting and scavenging nutrients once it could draw upon the sugars and waste products coming from its new photosynthesizing boarder.

Many species of these photosynthetic bacteria, cyanobacteria, exist as independent cells; others remain attached as they multiply, creating filamentous colonies. Cyanobacteria is the first living microorganism ever described by Antonie van Leeuwenhoek.
WIM VAN EGMOND

The novel dual-organism prospered. Some of its descendants went on to become algae, and the algae evolved into an assortment of forms. One of those gave rise to a type of vegetation able to colonize moist land (likely, biologists think, with the aid of a symbiotic fungus, since the proto-plant wouldn't yet have developed a root system of its own). In time, the colonists' offspring spread to drier sites and diversified through hundreds of millions of years, raising the percentage of oxygen in the air all the while. Some evolved into more advanced, flowering forms. One type became the ancestor of the rose family, and a member of that family went on to found the *Fragaria* line. And voilà! The strawberry.

While a small, single-celled alga may hold only one chloroplast, typical flowering plants contain anywhere from twenty

to a hundred in each cell of their leaves and stem. If you can't quite believe these green "organelles" are bacteria, pretend a microbiologist is showing you a chloroplast at super-high magnification. You'll notice that it comes with its own DNA. This genetic material, the chromosome, is arranged in a circle and is not contained within a nucleus, two traits found only in bacteria and archaea. The chloroplast's genes don't resemble those of the host plant, and the chloroplast produces its own descendants by dividing independently of the host cell that contains it.

As with any organism, the photosynthetic bacteria coexisting within plant cells are subject to occasional mutations. Natural selection now favored the variations best adapted to survival within the gooey protoplasm of another organism. (In fact, some of the bacteria's functions came to be influenced by genes in the host's nucleus over time, making chloroplasts more and more reliant upon the cells they inhabit.) As the chloroplasts kept evolving over time, they became so unlike the original cyanobacteria that the possibility of these "organelles" being actual organisms themselves didn't occur to earlier biologists. Finally, twentieth-century researchers were able to trace the chloroplasts' ancestry through molecular analyses that showed how the genes and enzymes were most closely related to those in bacteria. The results confirmed that a joint venture between two organisms, believed to have begun hundreds of millions of years before the earliest complex multicellular organisms appeared on Earth, went on to become a priceless boon to the entire spectrum of plants that arose, to every plant-eater, and to every eater of plant-eaters.

Back to basic biology class: a different organelle, the mitochondrion, is present inside almost every cell of virtually every life form except bacteria and archaea. Often described as the powerhouses of cells, mitochondria conduct organic compounds through a series of reactions to build the molecule adenosine triphosphate, or ATP. When other processes break ATP's tight chemical bonds, the considerable energy released is what drives cell metabolism, movement, and growth. If you go looking for the source of the spark of life, ATP is about as close as you can get.

adenosine triphosphate
ah-den-no-scene
try-foss-fate

Depending on its placement and function within an organism, a cell will typically have somewhere between a handful of mitochondria and a couple hundred. In the multitasking human liver, some cells have more than 2,000. The role of these organelles in cell activities is so central that neither a human nor a strawberry nor any other life form you can see—or almost any of the invisible protists and fungi—would exist without them. Like chloroplasts, mitochondria have their own DNA, which is different from that of the host cell, and they divide to reproduce independently of that cell. When molecular biologists analyzed mitochondrial genes, they found that, sure enough, the hereditary material is most similar to that of certain bacteria (even though, as with chloroplasts, some of the mitochondria's genes came to be incorporated within the DNA of their host cells through the ages).

Once again, it looks as though far, far back in the days when almost everybody on Earth was only one cell big, a bacterium got slurped into a larger microbe and, instead of being digested, ended up forming an alliance, perhaps because it gave the mini-predator a little extra energy jolt. The relationship may have developed by some other means, but however it formed, it turned into a symbiosis ubiquitous across the living planet. Being powered by the modified bacteria called mitochondria adds greatly to the definition of our greater selves. It means that there is far more to being human and more to the qualities we share with strawberries and all other multicellular creatures, as well as with the protists and single-celled fungi, than most people have ever bothered to think about. But maybe now you will. Of course, giving a nod to your mitochondria, recognizing how jammed full you are of miniature battery beings, isn't going to make you look different in the mirror tomorrow. It doesn't put you under any obligation to stop using the word I either. As for the mitochondria, it doesn't matter to them what you do or what you think you are as long as you stay healthy.

NEXT SPREAD

(Definition) Wild strawberry: the supremely edible, crimson result of sunlight processed with genetic instructions from an entire community of life.
ANNA BRADLEY

Coda to a Strawberry

So, pray tell, what is a strawberry? The answer is: more—more creatures linked in more ways—than anyone in all the earlier generations of humans bending down to pluck toothsome red fruits from this plant could possibly have envisioned. After the Dutch lens-maker and self-taught scientist Antonie van Leeuwenhoek fashioned the first microscope able to bring microbes into focus, he named the tiny spheres, rods, and squiggling spirals "animalcules" and accurately guessed that the number of such organisms in his mouth was greater than the number of people dwelling in the Netherlands. Though secretive about his lens-making technique and observation methods, he sent accurately rendered drawings of these animalcules together with written descriptions of details to the esteemed Royal Society in 1673. The response from some members was essentially, "Thanks for sharing your fantasies, weirdo." They were sure Anton had

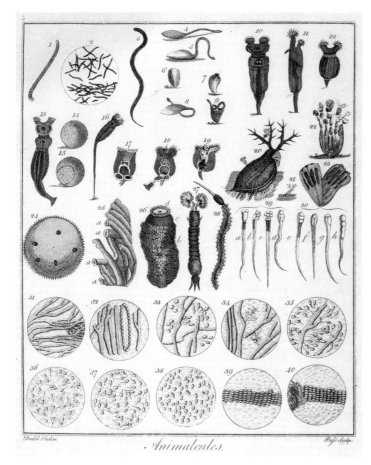

In the mid-1600s, Dutch lens-maker Antonie van Leeuwenhoek sent leading scientists illustrations of the life forms he saw with the high-power microscope he had invented. Experts dismissed them as figments of a feverish imagination. ARTIST UNKNOWN/ALAMY PHOTO

. Animalcules.

got carried away imagining that these odd, almost impossibly small motes could be living things.

After recognizing van Leeuwenhoek's contributions later on, scientists named the wee-est of the wee beasties "bacteria." But nobody had much of a clue about the roles such organisms played in nature for most of the next two centuries. It was 1835 when a scientific paper by Italian entomologist Agostino Bassi first suggested that microorganisms might be a cause of disease

CHAPTER ELEVEN

in larger creatures, and decades passed before Louis Pasteur and Robert Koch clearly linked certain microbial species with the process of fermentation and others with illness in humans.

More decades rolled by before biologists grasped that bacteria—still thought of by much of the public today as unwelcome germs—are far and away the most numerous, diverse, and pervasive life forms on Earth and do a nearly infinite number of things other than ferment or spoil food and cause disease. As for chloroplasts and mitochondria representing ancient lines of bacteria, the subject remained controversial in scientific circles as recently as the 1980s—more than a decade after America had landed people on the moon. That those all-important symbioses finally became accepted as facts was due in large part to a brilliant and strong-willed evolutionary biologist named Lynn Margulis, who advanced the concepts in the face of criticism and ridicule from many of her colleagues. As for the role of *Methylobacterium* in producing the strawberry's flavor, that was only discovered several years ago as science itself continues to grow and evolve.

. . .

As many as 20,000 species of lichens cover roughly 6 percent of Earth's land surface. Attaching themselves to raw soil, rocks, wood, and leaves, they grow in forms ranging from thin films resembling stains to tiny colorful cups raised on pedestals to thick, leaf-like clusters and long draperies hanging from plant branches. Lichens were generally considered types of plants themselves until the Swiss botanist Simon Schwendener examined them carefully through a microscope and declared instead that he was looking at a combination of a fungus and algae.

In a Costa Rican cloud forest, a lichen katydid (Markia hystrix) camouflaged on its favorite food source, a species of beard lichen (Usnea). MICHAEL AND PATRICIA FOGDEN/ MINDEN PICTURES

A petrified dune formation on the Colorado Plateau in Arizona holds dark concretion balls in a fracture line above swirls etched over the centuries by mineral-seeking lichens. JACK DYKINGA/ MINDEN PICTURES

That was in 1867. All too predictably, the first reaction of many prominent, experts invested in previous ideas was to scorn Schwendener and dismiss his discovery of a symbiosis. Their belief that organisms are autonomous, each existing as a separate and unique unit of life, was the very bedrock of the way they classified and compartmentalized nature.

Decades passed before Schwendener's notion of a dual organism became more widely adopted. As the years rolled on and microscope technology continued to improve, researchers found that the partners within the fungal webwork of a lichen are sometimes single-celled algae, sometimes cyanobacteria, and sometimes both at once. Many lichens contain other species of bacteria as well, and there turns out to be not just one kind of fungus involved but nearly always two different kinds. The second belongs to a different division of the fungal kingdom that went largely ignored in lichens until 2016, when it was identified as a regular partner by Toby Spribille, a University of Montana researcher at the time.

Prior to the nineteenth century, mycorrhizal fungi were thought to be parasitic molds that afflicted the roots of certain vegetation. As with lichens, botanists only gradually—it might be fair to say grudgingly—came to realize they were looking at a partnership helpful to both types of organisms. Even then, many continued to regard such root-and-fungus fusions as one of nature's oddities. During the second half of the twentieth century, having uncovered a variety of forms of this mutualism and detected mycorrhizae in nearly every plant family and more than 80 percent of all the plant species examined, scientists at last accepted this flora-plus-fungi symbiosis as the rule rather than the exception in nature. These days, when I look at a leafy

As much—if not more—of a forest grows underground as above the soil. In prairies and savannas, almost 90 percent of the grasses' mass lies in their deep, wide-spreading root systems. Artwork originally commissioned for Emergence Magazine.
KATIE HOLTEN

CODA TO A STRAWBERRY

green plant rising from the ground, I tend to visualize it as a composite life form somewhat resembling a lichen, for even the grandest tree consists of a webwork of fungi in symbiosis with a population of photosynthesizing cells (which in turn contain symbiotic bacteria in the form of choloroplasts and mitochondria). The difference is that the tree's main fungal partner, the web of mycorrhizae interwoven with the roots, stays out of sight underfoot rather than enclosing its photosynthesizing partner as fungi do in a lichen.

Botanists have known for a while that plants communicate by broadcasting hormones and other chemical signals through the air. The messages may say something about the sender's condition, for example, "I'm getting ready to flower." This can possibly stimulate members of the same species in the area to adjust their development so that they flower in synchrony, maximizing their chances of being pollinated by one another. Or the molecules wafting through the forest may carry the news, "I'm under attack" (by wood-boring beetles or a rust fungus, etc.). Receiving what amounts to a warning from the victim, nearby plants of the same species will begin increasing their production of chemicals designed to deter the invaders.

Once the botanists began looking underground, they found plants communicating opportunities and warnings through their root and fungal networks too. White cedar and maize are two examples of plants whose root systems, when under assault from insects, manufacture chemicals that spread out through the groundwater, the mycorrhizae, or both and recruit insect-eating nematodes to the roots. The more ecologists search, the more types of messages they discover being sent and received via what they are beginning to recognize as a colossal subterranean internet linking plants of the same species and sometimes of different species. And they find that what's being exchanged is not only chemical information but nutrients as well—from mother plants to offspring, healthy plants to ailing plants, and so on.

Lichens are among the longest-lived entities on the planet. Although still named and classified as if they were distinct species, all appear to be composites of at least three different organisms—five, if you count the mitochondria and chloroplasts representing ancient bacteria. Exactly how to define those self-contained communities is a question scientists have yet to settle. Some have switched from defining a lichen as a symbiosis to labeling it a holobiont, the more accurate term for the multicreature collaboration. If you think about a strawberry, the holobiont label also fits. As I mentioned in an earlier chapter, the label applies fairly well to most other visible creatures too.

For that matter, the concept of a holobiont could be expanded to describe the interdependent contents and connections that make up a large-scale community or ecosystem such as a forest, a savanna, or a marsh. Is that exaggerating the definition of an organism or sheer fantasy? Or is it an incentive to think about every aspect of nature as something greater and alive in more ways than we were able to make sense of before? I'm going to go with the last option.

· · ·

After describing a strawberry's elaborate reproductive strategy involving flowers, nectars, pollen, pollinators, alluring fruits, seeds, and seed dispersers, it's time to consider *Fragaria's* ability to make more of itself without that whole apparatus. It does so by the asexual, or vegetative, method of natural cloning. Once

daily temperatures begin to rise above 50 degrees Fahrenheit during the growing season, a mature strawberry plant will start sending out bright red horizontal runners across the ground. As gardeners know, where a runner makes ample contact with the soil, a bud may form and generate the roots, vertical stem, and leaves of an identical plant.

A reevaluation of what we consider to be an individual life form would seem to be in order. Whole groves of elms or aspens, acres of bunchgrass in prairies, groups of mosses or onions, cholla cactus thickets, daffodil clusters, and a broad assortment of other plants you come upon as groups may in fact be collections of clones. Many types of vegetation can propagate asexually either

by surface runners (also called stolons), creeping rootstocks (rhizomes), or lateral roots (suckers) that grow from the main root and then where they penetrate the surface, become separate-looking stems or trunks. Other types of vegetation replicate themselves from buds that develop on underground bulbs and tubers or else generate packets of tissue on branches or leaf margins that fall to the ground to take root. The plants that result not only have genes identical to those of the single parent but are also likely to be transferring nutrients between one clone and the next through interwoven root systems and also the shared network of mycorrhizae attached to the roots. Where in this scene is there a solitary, independent, or otherwise separate organism—an individual?

Parthenogenesis, the production of female offspring by females that have not been fertilized by a male, occurs in some worms, mollusks, crustaceans, scorpions, insects, and an assortment of smaller invertebrates. It also takes place among the vertebrates in certain fish, amphibians, and reptiles from finger-size lizards to giant Komodo dragons. This, too, is usually a form of cloning, for the "mother" is essentially just copying herself. It's the bigger-critter version of a single-celled organism simply dividing in two, the animal equivalent of a strawberry plant sending out runners to replicate its roots and leaves in a different spot.

The social insects include familiar species of bees and wasps and nearly all ants and termites. (Among the most numerous, successful insects on Earth, termites are well-known for relying on microbes in their gut to digest the wood they devour. The symbiotic microbes are mainly protists, part of that broad spectrum of single-celled organisms with a nucleus. Not long ago, researchers realized that the wood-digesting enzymes protists contribute actually come from symbiotic bacteria living on the surface of the protists' cell membrane or even inside the protists.) In most social insect colonies, one fertilized animal, the queen, can produce tremendous numbers of sterile female offspring. With worker and soldier castes of different sizes and shapes programmed to carry out different activities such as defense, food-gathering, caring for eggs and larvae, or tending to her majesty, the colony becomes a sort of automated society.

In many respects, the highly organized division of labor among the various castes in a social insect colony resembles the functions of the different specialized cells making up various organs

of a larger
animal's body.
   Considering the colony
as a life form in its own right
begins to seem reasonable. After all,
the evolutionary unit is not the singular
moving part we identify as "an ant," "this termite," "that bee," etc., most of which cannot even breed.
It is the colony as a whole that competes for resources,
grows or shrinks, is subject to natural selection, and changes
over time as a result. Following the lead of the renowned
entomologist and population ecologist Edward O. Wilson,
some scientists speak of complex social insect colonies with
highly efficient communication networks as superorganisms.
A social insect colony tends to exert an influence on its
environment many times greater than the same number
of insects could have acting independently.

   Weaver ants are found in the tropical forests of
Africa, Southeast Asia, northeastern
Australia, and Melanesia. They are
named for their trait of stitching
leaves together into ball-shaped
nests using silk from the colony's
larvae. These ants also protect scale
insects from enemies and harvest special
nutrient-rich droplets that the scale insects exude while feeding
on plant juices. It is a quasi-symbiotic relationship similar to the
one other ants have with flocks of aphids they tend. (Aphids have
their own symbiosis with the bacterium *Buchnera aphidicola*.
Housed in special cells called bacteriocytes, *Buchnera* receive

nutrients from the aphids and in return supply the insects with
ants hundreds of essential amino acids they can't make for themselves. The more
thousands strong op-
erates as a complex closely you examine organisms of almost every kind, the more
civilization. Here, symbioses you find.)
nonbreeding workers
form living chains   Though of ordinary size and very lightweight, weaver ants
to pull leaves into also hunt other insects and cooperate to subdue prey up to the
position. Other work-
ers follow to stitch size of scorpions and small lizards. With their combination of
the edges together, hyperaggressive behavior, a potent bite magnified by formic
forming a large
ball-shaped nest for acid, sheer numbers, and rapid information transfer through
the queen. MARK chemical signaling, weaver ants are capable of dominating the
MOFFETT/MINDEN
PICTURES forest canopies where they live, driving off competing insects
and even fair-size birds and mammals. Consisting almost
entirely of nonbreeding females, colonies may have half a million members, enough that some can be found patrolling nearly
every leaf for a hundred feet or more around the queen's nest.

On assignment for *National Geographic* magazine in the rainforest of northeastern Australia, I spent a couple weeks observing weaver ants with Mark Moffett, a top-ranked nature photographer. He also happens to be a theoretical ecologist and trained entomologist who gets introduced as "Dr. Bugs" when he makes appearances on national television in the United States. Moffett wanted to test relations between neighboring weaver colonies, and he had been making long-distance phone calls to Edward O. Wilson, his former adviser at Harvard, to discuss the design of an experiment we planned to carry out. While Moffett and I looked over a likely site, I leaned in to peer a little more closely at one weaver ant soldier poised on a leaf's outer edge. She took offense. Releasing an alarm scent, she recruited hundreds of companions that came racing with open jaws from the nearest leaves in a matter of seconds. Within a couple of minutes, tens of thousands more were streaming my way in solid lines stretching from several of the nearest trees. At which point I was already doing the pants-on-fire rainforest boogie, dancing away while brushing off the ants swarming and biting my face and every other part of me.

The members of a weaver ant colony, in total, may weigh no more than a single monkey—or, in Australia and New Guinea rainforests, a tree kangaroo (yes, there are around a dozen such climbing species). Yet the colony's presence is all-encompassing, as if that monkey or tree 'roo dissolved into gel and spread out as a biofilm, a thin, sensitive coating over all the surfaces of the colony's territory. I am here to testify that infringing on their claim to the place hurts like hell. I saw it get a lot worse for any trespassing weaver with the scent of a foreign colony. She would be grabbed by a squad of defenders, stretched out, chewed on where her armor was weakest, and literally taken apart. And if the alarm pheromones she gave off during her encounter brought in a column of her colony sisters, the border clash that ensued might quickly escalate to massive warfare with thousands of deaths. Yet the overall cost to the colonies was limited by the fact that as weaver ants age and their physical abilities diminish, they move to the fringes of a territory to serve as the colony's first line of defense. Or as another entomologist observed, whereas human societies rely heavily on young men to fill the ranks of their armies, with weaver ants it's mostly the "old ladies" that get sent off to the war front.

. . .

What is one nonbreeding female warrior in a weaver ant colony? What do we call the giant, jellyfish-like Portuguese man o' war, which is in reality a siphonophore, a very large colony of cloned animals organized a bit like a social insect hive, with different members performing quite different tasks such as catching prey, digestion, and reproduction? What about corals or giant clams? Both are animals, yet both are intimately tied to various species of algae—and often cyanobacteria as well—that live within their tissues and produce nutrients for their hosts through photosynthesis. The same can be said of various sea sponges, a large number of sea slugs (technically called nudibranchs, meaning naked gills), and a great many other soft-bodied marine animals. Examples of symbionts and/or holobionts stretch far and wide across the vast kingdom of multicellular organisms, and more are being recognized by the year.

And now, pray tell, what is that person over there who happens to be eating a strawberry? Not a human clone—not yet,

siphonophore
sai-faa-nuh-for

nudibranch
noo-dee-branch

CHAPTER ELEVEN

Nembrotha cristata, a nudibranch, or sea slug, offshore Sulawesi, Indonesia. Some nudibranchs have marine algae living in their tissues as symbionts producing extra food. Others graze algae whose symbiotic bacteria produce toxins that, once absorbed by the slug, make it distasteful to predators. DRAY VAN BEECK/ MINDEN PICTURES

though it may be only a matter of time. (Nearly two dozen mammal species have been cloned so far. Among the latest, in 2018, were a pair of crab-eating macaque monkeys, which share something like 93 percent of our genes.) Not really a unit of a superorganism either. Human societies with a rigid social caste system and enforced division of labor have come close to meeting the definition of operating as giant colonial creatures. But our behavior is too varied and flexible—especially in regard to the sublime vagaries of love that affect who ends up mating with whom—to fit the superorganism category. Nevertheless, like the strawberry and every other multicellular organism, *Homo sapiens* qualifies as more than a symbiont. So I'll repeat the theme again: hosting a long list of mutualist life forms whether we realize that or not, dependent for food on a long list of mutualist plants and animals whether we think of them that way or not, we are holobionts whether we're ready for that label or not.

Alright, so picture yourself chatting away with somebody. Let's arbitrarily make this someone a male; the chances are close to 50-50 in most human populations. Let's further suppose you bring up an environmental or wildlife issue. He listens with a polite expression as you speak. Then—while living with trillions of microbes inside, many of them busy providing him with go-power and digestive abilities and defending him against disease; while more microbes are in and on everything he eats and everything he touches; while he exhales tens of thousands with each breath and has tens of thousands more drifting off his skin; while he moves around in that microbial mist interacting with the live personal mists of every person and pet in the vicinity; while he is nourished, oxygenated, and influenced in countless other ways by organisms large and small, underfoot and overhead, close by and all around the only living planet we know—this person offers a palms-up shrug and says, "To tell the truth, I'm really just not all that into nature."

He is as human as a human can be and is at the same time a walking, talking ecosystem—a smartphone-operating, grocery-shopping, dreaming one moment and credit card-swiping the next, traffic-jam-hating, surely strawberry-shortcake-loving, music-playing carrier of universally shared genes and the host for a collection of microbiomes. Lacking the invisible hordes normally inhabiting his mouth and guts and skin, he might survive for a while—in a bubble with artificial life support. Lacking mitochondria, he would die. So you'd only be telling him the truth straight-up if you replied, "Well, nature is not really what you think it is, you're not really what you think you are, and you're only around because nature is totally into you." But get ready. An awkward silence might follow ... and last a while.

An artist commissioned to illustrate the way many folks think about our position in the living world might paint a scene with us as the shining capstone atop a grand pyramid of species. Instead, the growing collection of revelations from recent studies sticks humankind within a tangled skein of other life forms. You, every friend, enemy, lover, dignitary, and desperado along with every other animal, every plant, and every fungus you'll ever meet, exist as a union. This doesn't refer to being the product of two parents. It means each of us is by nature a collaboration or collective—a joint venture—of fellow Earthlings.

Our newly realized position doesn't undermine our prowess and potential, doesn't make us any less amazing. Our spectrum of biological relationships makes us more than human. And being human was already pretty marvelous, for we possess an extraordinary brand of imaginative intelligence coupled with social mechanisms for sharing and building upon information that appear to be unrivaled. So, make of those qualities all you will. But for goodness' sake don't look for insight from anybody not particularly interested in the fate of nature on a living planet, much less willing to do something about it. That holobiont missed the memo to Know Thyself.

Crowboarding

With a warm sun on your shoulders and a bundle of luck, you might see a grizzly bear go sliding down a leftover snowbank and then climb up to the starting point and take another slide— or three. I watched a mother grizz do that, sledding downslope on her back over and over again while holding two cubs on her chest. I've also seen mountain goats and mountain sheep run and glissade down steep summer snowfields, with the goats sometimes adding leaps, bucks, horn-tosses, and midair spins like rodeo bulls just out of the chute. In Russia, a man named Aleksey Vnukov filmed a European crow repeatedly riding down a snowy rooftop, using a plastic can lid like a snowboard. He put the video up on YouTube, and some commenter promptly named the sport "crowboarding."

In tropical New Caledonia, the crows use long, thin twigs held in their beaks to extract insect larvae from holes. Crows belong to the same big-brained family of songbirds as ravens, and ravens turn the word *birdbrain* from a slur into a compliment. Although they sometimes go sliding down snow headfirst to clean their feathers after feeding on a carcass, their body-sledding at other times seems to be mainly for entertainment. We're talking about birds that will snap off a twig from a high tree branch, purposefully drop it, fly down to catch the thing in midair, wing back up, drop it, and catch it again, doing this over and over like a dog that figured out how to throw a ball for itself.

Ravens unzip backpack pockets to snitch food. They'll lift up seat cushions on snowmobiles to grab a lunch from the storage compartment underneath. When the sledheads (as snowmobile enthu-siasts call themselves) tie a rope across the seat to keep the cover

Like chimpanzees are known to do, this Hawaiian crow uses a stick to probe for insects. New Caledonian crows go a step further, breaking off a twig to the length needed to probe cavities and trimming away its branches and leaves. ZSSD/MINDEN PICTURES

227

closed, ravens untie the knots. Some that overwinter in the Arctic have learned to shroud village streetlamps with their wings so the sensors will register darkness during the day and turn on the lights, which give off welcome heat.

When I observed a raven in Yellowstone National Park tug on a wolf's tail to distract the mammal from a carcass so the bird could flap in and grab a morsel for itself, I was impressed but not really surprised. In an aviary at his home in New England, Bernd Heinrich, a student of ravens for many years, had earlier told me of experiments in which he presented birds with meat dangling from a string tied to their perch. Crows would reach down and pull the string up as far as they could, but it was never enough to bring the meat within reach. His wild-caught ravens briefly looked over the situation and then pulled up a section of the string, stood on it so the weight of the meat wouldn't cause it to slip back down, pulled up another length, stood on that, and continued the routine until they had the reward in their beak.

Captive chimpanzees and grizzly bears will pile up objects to climb on in order to reach a food reward overhead. Elephants held in a compound stacked logs against one of the walls and placed their front feet up on them to reach tree branches with tasty leaves that had been too high to grab with their trunk before. In a different compound, a honey badger kept climbing sticks or trees near the enclosure's walls to escape. Recaptured and finding that every last bit of wood had been removed from its living space, this honey badger escape artist worked wet soil into balls, rolled them into a corner, and stacked them up high enough against the wall to break out again.

Japanese macaques, popularly called snow monkeys, pack snowballs and roll those atop sticky snow to create larger balls for no apparent purpose other than amusement. Researchers studying this species watched the behavior of washing food in water gradually spread through a troop after a single animal began removing sand from a sweet potato that way rather than brushing off the grit with the back of its hand. In Southeast Asia, crab-eating macaques use favorite stones to crack open nuts, snails, and crabs and also to dislodge oysters tightly attached to surfaces. It's probably safe to assume that these uses of a tool were "invented" by a single animal in a social group and later adopted by other members and eventually by other troops observing them. Elephant matriarchs lead their herds to dry-season waterholes they learned about from older female leaders, and the younger females paying attention will one day do the same. In an Australian bay, bottlenose dolphin females teach their daughters the trick of carrying around marine sponges to place as padding over their snouts when they nose after prey hidden in rough seafloor debris.

Like the stone-carrying macaques, sea otters often tote around a favorite rock, which they use to smash open urchins and mollusks. And like the New Caledonian crows, Galápagos finches employ toothpick-like sticks for spearing insects deep in crannies. Elephants will grab a length of wood with their trunk and use it to scratch themselves in an otherwise hard-to-reach spot. On Alaska's coast, a grizzly was observed sorting through barnacle-encrusted rocks and finally selecting one that fit its paw just right and then putting it to work giving itchy spots an extra-hard scratching.

But what are we to make of the small octopus toting around half of a coconut shell and using it as a protective dome to hide under in the presence of predators? There's always the happy accident factor when it comes to novel behaviors that qualify as the use of a tool, which is to say that while necessity may be the mother of invention, just goofing and fiddling around with stuff is surely one of the fathers. So, was this an octopus that had just experienced its own *Eureka!* moment? Or had it previously found a large seashell to hide under and adapted the technique after coming upon the lighter coconut husk on the ocean floor? Or did that little animal with eight nimble arms give the coconut husk a try after seeing another octopus do something similar?

I mentioned the concept of a meme in an earlier chapter. The term defines a discrete behavior that is transmitted from one individual to another through learning and may be passed along from one generation to the next. Insofar as the behavior improves a creature's chances of surviving and producing off-spring, a meme, like a gene, can fan out through a population and influence the evolution of that species.

For example, social groups of killer whales, or orcas, along the Pacific Northwest coast developed different habits related to the type and whereabouts of the prey they favored. The habits became learned traditions within the groups. Today in the northern Pacific, resident killer whales travel in fairly large pods and strictly eat fish; smaller, stealthier transient orca pods only hunt mammals such as seals, sea lions, dolphins, porpoises, and larger whales; while offshore orcas, which form the largest pods, roam the continental shelf apparently taking sharks as well as schools of fish. These preferences for particular food sources and accompanying hunting strategies became associated with dif-ferences in the calls and songs each type of killer whale uses to communicate within its own society. The groups now speak in quite different languages.

Aboard research boats with hydrophones in the water, I quickly learned to tell which sort of killer whales we were eavesdropping on. Even when the different types happen to find themselves in the same general area, they avoid each other and socialize only with their own kind. This cultural isolation—a preference for companions, including mates, that behave and sound most like themselves—produces results much like those that develop in populations that become geographically separated. Over time, they may become different ecotypes and eventually distinct races or subspecies. Genetic analyses show that the different types of killer whales I mentioned have not interbred for thousands of years. Millennia of natural selection have made the culturally distinct groups dissimilar enough in their physical appearance for experienced observers to readily tell them

Known as the veined octopus or, these days, the coconut octopus, Amphioctopus marginatus *lives in tropical Indo-Asian waters. It went viral on social media after one was videoed carrying around half a coconut husk to hide under in the presence of predators.* MIKE VEITCH/ALAMY PHOTO

apart when the animals surface for air. Some authorities think the ecotypes have already become separate species, whether or not science is ready to officially recognize them as such.

People assume that we big-brained humans live life at a higher level than other organisms are capable of—that we enjoy a richness of existence unlike any other creature experiences either mentally or emotionally. Despite being unsure of how consciousness forms or where it resides or, for that matter, exactly what it is, we pride ourselves on possessing this quality and have generally refused to attribute more than a primitive version of it

An orca pod in the clear cold waters off Norway. Highly social, most remain in tight family groups from birth to death, a span of eighty years or more. These are dolphins with a brain weighing four times as much as a human's.
PAUL NICKLEN

to any other species. Maybe that's justified, yet maybe it's only the cherished opinion of an intensely self-aware primate.

Since this book is about the factual nature of nature, I should point out that the brains of killer whales (and for the record, they are huge dolphins) are also highly developed and can be up to four times as large as ours. Adult male sperm whale brains are as much as six times as big as human brains. Most of the other great whales' brains also exceed a person's in size. The brains of elephants are roughly three times the size of ours. Many experts as well as laypeople have traditionally focused on the brain-to-body weight ratio rather than sheer brain size as an indicator of intelligence. It ranks us back above those chunky elephants and blubbery whales, though only a fraction above many dolphins. But relying on this ratio to gauge smarts sets us below some small rodents and several types of little featherlight birds. Just sayin'.

· · ·

Over the past decade, the term *meme* has increasingly become used to mean a lifestyle trend, an attitude, a catchy expression or slogan, or just about any other human practice in the process of becoming way cool and widely copied. In that sense, meme refers to something more fleeting than animal behavior researchers intended, since it may not last long enough to be passed from one generation to the next. Still, both uses of the word meet the definition of "the social transmission of learned information."

The fascinating aspect of many memes in current human cultures is the speed at which they sweep along via modern electronic communications. We're primarily a visual species, and these days we have countless extra eyes and storage space for images in the form of the mobile phones now carried by more than half the humans on Earth teenaged or older. More eyes proliferate in the form of stationary video monitors set out in the countryside and automatic cameras mounted on helmets, dashboards, remotely controlled land vehicles, drones, and submersibles. All of them are observing the world on our behalf. With added options and better resolution every year, these robo-eyes keep multiplying our contact with one another and, importantly, with all kinds of creatures.

Although we have an ever-expanding universe of digitized subject matter to choose from, our ordinary household

companions, cats and dogs, claim an inordinate amount of space on the web. An addiction to cat videos has become a meme in itself. Native creatures recorded in their natural habitats keep running wild all over the internet too. Whatever else the instant global communication that defines our era might be praised or criticized for, it has clearly demonstrated a strong and abiding fascination with animals. Press a button, the smartphone or computer screen lights up, and there they are: Earthlings of all shapes and sizes, the glorious and the bizarre, performing astonishing athletic feats or elaborate courtship rituals. Snagging prey. Caring for young. Playing with companions or just acting wacky. Keeping unlikely company with neighboring species or

Warm hearts in a fiercely cold realm. Extended care and a long learning period for the young are invaluable strategies for polar bear survival. Some cubs continue to nurse for the entire two-and-a-half years they stay with Mom.
FLORIAN SCHULZ

curiously interacting with people. And doing a thousand other things that open windows into their lives and psyches.

Interpreting the motives and behavior of animals has always been one of the toughest challenges in biology. It wasn't so long ago that supposedly clear-thinking scientists were still binge-profiling other species as "beasts," "brutes," "mere animals," etc.—and similarly dismissing entire human races and societies as "primitive" and "inferior." After that, the scientific community took a different approach: to embrace behavioral models that portrayed virtually all other animals, including highly intelligent mammalian kin, as little more than hardwired stimulus-response machines on autopilot, rigidly ruled by instincts.

Today's experts have expanded their views well beyond the old patronizing and mechanistic schemes. Researchers are now willing to describe the vocalizations of certain whales and primates, a bird's repertoire of calls and songs, a prairie dog's vocabulary of whistles, and even the sequence in which an ant displays different postures and emits certain scents as variations on language. Yet when drawing conclusions about things animals "say," it is the scientists themselves who remain somewhat tongue-tied, hedging every point they make with "if's," "and's," and "but's" while couching their results in strenuously neutral analytical jargon. They do this in part to skirt the risk of slipping into anthropomorphism—attributing human characteristics to animals. Even though one of the most common phrases you'll find in professional publications about animal behavior nowadays is "... a quality formerly considered unique to humans ... ", science still lacks a comfortable framework and terminology for discussing behavior that blurs the boundary between animals' capabilities and those we have traditionally reserved for ourselves.

All of which emphasizes how difficult it is for humans to sidestep prevailing cultural opinions and their own personal mindsets in order to see another creature, a differently designed being, objectively. To break through barriers, sometimes you first have to get out of your own damn way, and that's tough for us self-referencing anthropos to do. In many respects, earlier human societies living close to nature seem to have understood humankind's kinship with other creatures more clearly than most modern societies have been able to do. Some considered various animals to be ancestors, while some saw them more as different kinds of tribes—the wolf people, for instance, the elephant people, or the fish people, each with their own language and customs, their own ways of interacting and doing things, their own moods, and their own yearnings.

Any number of Indigenous groups maintain these traditions to some degree. I've found myself thinking how recent research in biology points less and less toward the concept of a pyramid-like hierarchy of creatures with us reigning at the top than toward the view shared by various Native American tribes that every type of being occupies an equal place on what amounts to a great Circle of Life, all of them linked to one another by that arrangement. While science continues to struggle with its convoluted definitions of the qualities we share with other creatures, much of the work to put the public in touch with animal emotions and learning abilities is being done by the internet and social media. And those electronic systems aren't even trying. Instead of burdening the material on view with attempts to explain it, most sites are content to simply post intriguing photos and video footage and let them speak for themselves.

I met the little octopus and its portable coconut shell armor while cruising the web to find tips for repairing my car. Millions of people saw that animal as well, just as millions watched the rooftop bird in Russia go crowboarding. All of us can digitally roam to our hearts' content from one animal to the next—and often do. Sure, we're usually just sitting on our butts and physically far removed from the subjects as we scroll around a backlit screen. And, you bet, some of the website offerings of animal behavior seem staged or otherwise questionable. Yet most are—*click*—simply there, random, uncomplicated, and fun for viewers to interpret any way they want.

If all someone learns from watching is "Whoa! This animal did *that!*" expectations are being changed. Take the number of instantly intriguing, nature-related postings appearing on the web 24/7 and multiply it by thousands of viewers around the world. That sum represents one of the most powerful and persuasive social changes revising humankind's attitudes toward nonhuman beings.

I don't want to drift too far into sociology, but I can't help but notice a strengthening of the movement to treat fellow creatures more humanely. Though hardly new, the trend appears to be expanding in parallel with the coverage given animals in both popular media and social media. People have been communicating at an intuitive level with domestic animals for ages. But as paying closer attention to their emotions became more acceptable and widely communicated, more pet owners found themselves noticing just how many subtly different degrees of exuberance, anxiety, attachment, and despondency those companions can express. Quite a few folks have bought books and watch programs about how to understand what their dog (cat, horse, etc.) is telling them.

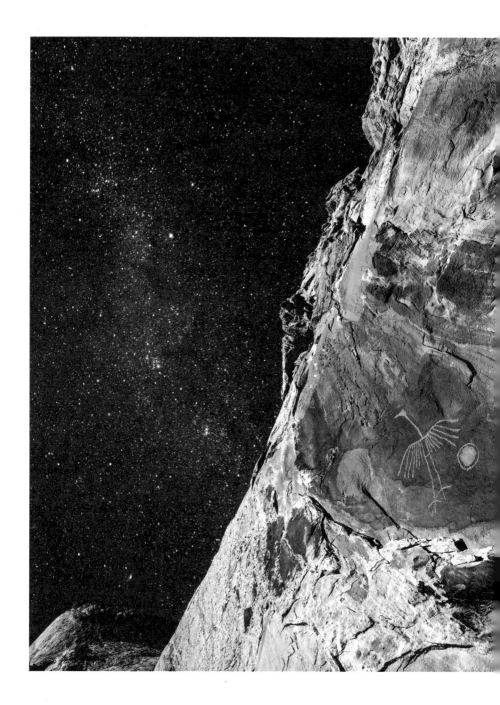

Ancient aboriginal rock art depicting a person with animals inside symbolizes the influence of nature on culture since humankind's earliest days.
CHRISTINA SPEED

And researchers have grown a little more open to at least offering guarded speculations about emotional states and consciousness in their wild subjects without worrying quite so much that colleagues might accuse them of having veered off the rails.

It's always going to be problematic to draw a line between the projection of our own thoughts and feelings onto animals and a genuine recognition of other species' cognitive abilities and emotions. Nevertheless, the philosophical barriers many societies had in place for differentiating humankind from animalkind are increasingly being breached, website by website, pet by household pet, and wildlife case study by wildlife case study. The change in attitude is translating into action on a number of fronts.

Most regions in the United States and many in other nations now have privately funded, largely volunteer-run centers for rehabilitating orphaned and injured wild animals. Growing numbers of people in outdoor clubs, civic youth programs, and school classes carry out citizen science studies and ecology projects such as rehabilitating streams and wetlands. Pressure from the public has led to some improvements in the quality of life for animals exhibited in circuses and zoos, those used for laboratory testing, and livestock raised in factory farms. Over the years, mainstream conservation organizations have expanded their focus from charismatic megafauna—big attractive animals with broad public appeal—to take in a much larger share of Earth's biological diversity, directing more attention to overlooked life forms whose roles within ecosystems are often equally, if not more, important. Think bats, bees, or ancient hardwood trees scheduled for removal in order to clear more room for a housing development. One way or another, all of those other Earthlings are knocking at humanity's door and asking to be allowed into our moral sphere.

NEXT SPREAD

Gorilla and caretaker share a moment at the Senkwekwe Center for orphaned gorillas in Virunga National Park, Democratic Republic of the Congo. JAMES GIFFORD

Although I can't predict where these efforts will lead, I know an extension of human empathy when I see it. And that force—simple kindness, altruism, compassion—keeps widening the cracks in long-established belief systems that proclaim humans to be separate and supreme creations somehow appointed to use all the rest of the living world however we wish. Given the mounting rate of losses within natural communities, a willingness to push through the myths and rationalizations that walled us off from other Earthlings is much-needed. It is also much-deserved as scientific advances continue to reveal unforeseen connections to the nature around and within us. Above all, it is hopeful.

... I know an extension of human empathy when I see it.

Why Y2Y?

The sages say, "The truth shall set you free." Author Joe Klass quoted this age-old proverb in his book *The Twelve Steps to Happiness*, adding, "... but first it will piss you off."

On the planet we all depend upon, much of the other life we know is being smothered by 7.8 billion-and-counting of us and the technology-amplified modern forces we've unleashed. That's the hard truth of the Anthropocene. The question I asked at the book's start was: What can any one of us do to change this era's trajectory? I promised suggestions. Rather than wander among the theories and debates about what people *ought* to be doing, I sought out practical projects that people *are* successfully doing right now. In the end I decided to just highlight two. The first is the far-reaching strategy for saving wildlife on oceanic islands described in chapters eight and nine. I kept the second project, one of the most effective large-scale conservation programs on the globe's continents, for this chapter near the book's end.

Around the same time biologists realized that our defini-tions of nature had been too limited, ecologists began to see

that the century-and-a-half-old practice of setting aside reserves here and there to safeguard nature was coming up short. It proved especially mismatched to the needs of big, mobile animals. Elephants, for example, and jaguars, wild camels, wolves, gazelles, bears, lions ... name one of the sizeable fellow mammals we find especially compelling and most want to save. When societies started establishing parks and preserves, much of the countryside around them remained more or less intact and able to provide important habitats at certain times of year and serve as travel routes to other vital habitats. That is no longer the case. Settlement and development have been fragmenting those landscapes, cutting reserves off from neighboring terrain and from each other. Many of the protected natural areas are turning into islands lapped by an ocean of humanity.

In twenty-first-century settings, animals traveling beyond refuges often struggle to find habitats with adequate food and security in adjoining terrain. Their chances for survival and reproduction there drop faster by the year. Increasingly isolated, the wildlife inside reserves becomes more susceptible to inbreeding and whatever natural disasters sweep through. Now add pressures from a global environment in the throes of a strong and accelerating warming trend. We already know that species on *oceanic* islands face an elevated risk of extinction. We also know that the smaller an island is and the farther away it lies from other areas with wildlife populations, the less variety of life it is able to support over time.

Most large land animals survived environmental changes over the ages by being able to migrate freely, flow back and forth between seasonal ranges, and readily relocate if conditions in an old homeland became less suitable. Having room for maturing members of a group to disperse and find new territories of their own has always been an important factor too. Where ready-to-roam species are able to meet potential mates from different locales and freshen depleted gene pools, recolonize areas that lost all or most of a resident population, and adapt to different predators and competitors across a broad region, communities of big wildlife will flourish. Where they no longer have those options, they're in trouble. Populations in a number of parks and preserves with inadequate acreage have already lost members or disappeared completely since those areas were first protected.

We owe earlier conservationists our praise for scrambling to save nature by placing intact chunks of it off-limits to most kinds of human disturbance. At the time, it wasn't clear that separate, scattered tracts could not by themselves fulfill the promise of preserving our natural heritage into the future. Hardly anyone foresaw how crowded and busy the world would soon be. That left present-day conservationists with a problem. But there is a fix for it: connections, the very same quality I've been examining throughout this book as the essence of living systems large and small.

If you want to see connectivity being built into a region's landscapes, you could grab a backpack and do some roaming of your own along the backbone of North America. There, you'll find the Yellowstone to Yukon Conservation Initiative (or Y2Y, as both the region and the organization are nicknamed) at work. Its goal is to conserve the 2,000-mile segment of the Continental Divide ecoregion that stretches from Wyoming's Wind River Range to the headwaters of the Peel River in Canada's Yukon Territory.

Audacious? By past standards, definitely. In terms of what we know about conservation now? It's what's called for. Look at

The Yellowstone to Yukon Conservation Initiative works to keep natural processes and wildlife communities intact for an ecoregion that runs north for 2,000 miles from northwestern Wyoming to headwaters of the Peel River in the Yukon.

the heritage at stake: half a million square miles of spectacular topography holding scores of reserves—among them, the world-renowned national parks of Grand Teton, Yellowstone, Glacier, Waterton Lakes, Banff, and Jasper. Y2Y is one of the very few large landscapes in a temperate climate zone that still has all of its native species. They include the greatest variety of wild plants in Canada and the highest diversity of big wild animals in North America. Not only have there been no extinctions recorded here, nearly all the region's flora and fauna are doing reasonably well, which is unusual anywhere on the globe nowadays.

Recognized wildland strongholds with prime habitats and unspoiled scenery form the cores, or focal areas, in Y2Y's design for regional conservation. Gaining protection for some of the biologically richest spots not already safeguarded as parks or preserves is part of the plan. The second part is securing connections— variously called linkage zones, habitat bridges, wildlife corridors, passageways, or just wildways—from one stronghold to the next, ideally through the least disturbed places left in between. The final part of Y2Y's mission embraces a necessary third dimension of connectivity in the Anthropocene: trying to blend conservation needs with the interests of local human communities.

The Initiative has more than 218 current partners in the United States and Canada. They include businesses, private landowners, Native American groups, scientists, resource institutes, and environmental organizations. It will take a coalition of this breadth to assemble a network of cores and varied connections that collectively operate as a meta-reserve across portions of two territories and two provinces in Canada and five US states. If this vision becomes a reality, the entire ecoregion could continue to function at nearly full strength as a natural system. Indefinitely. And if the network only gets partially completed, that may still be enough to keep the natural realm from having to keep giving way, again and again, until the remnants stand huddled in refuges where people go to see what used to run far, wide, and free.

Wild as ever, the Wind River flowing north out of the Mackenzie Mountains is just one of half a dozen equally spectacular big tributaries of the Peel River in the Yukon Territory.
PETER MATHER

In 1993, the year the Y2Y coalition was formally launched, its ambitions were viewed by some as pie-in-the-sky-class unrealistic and by others as a grave threat to the economy. Protected core areas made up 10 to 11 percent of the ecoregion at the time. A quarter of a century later, that figure has more than doubled. Some of the added acreage consists of new national parks and wilderness areas. Recently established buffer zones, special management areas, recreation areas, natural areas, ecological reserves, state and provincial parks, and similar administrative units within Y2Y's vast stockpile of public lands also count toward the core areas total. Although few of these other segments are as strictly

protected as a national park, the regulations governing them still provide an improved level of security for the native flora and fauna. The same holds true for various portions of public land given enough safeguards against unchecked development to help tie the core areas to one another. Land trusts contributed still more linkage acreage by arranging conservation easements with the owners of private properties. According to Y2Y's analysis, total connectivity along the length of the Yellowstone to Yukon landscape increased from 5 percent in 1993 to more than 30 percent today. Negotiations are underway to begin setting up Indigenous Protective Areas on treaty lands in Canada claimed by First Nations people. Since the Protective Areas are to be managed by the tribes to conserve traditional natural resources, they may soon add tremendous amounts of territory with improved management of the region's living resources.

. . .

Now I understand what the Initiative's first coordinator, Bart Robinson, meant when I asked him in the early 1990s what Y2Y was actually doing besides announcing worthy intentions, and he replied, "We're in year two of a hundred-year plan." He was telling me that a conservation effort at this whopping scale necessarily starts with wishful thinking. The Initiative did a lot of that in its early years and still does. Willful optimism, steadily supplied, can be contagious. It has already helped make Y2Y one of the best-conserved mountain ecosystems in the world, and we're still only in year twenty-eight as of 2021.

Another important transformation was taking place in much of the ecoregion during the same period. Recreation and tourism became major generators of jobs and revenue. The longstanding ideology that more protection for the environment hurts business started going the way of typewriters and rotary dial telephones as environmental progress and economic progress kept advancing arm in arm through districts from northern Wyoming well into British Columbia and Alberta. Figures from the Outdoor Industry Association recently showed outdoor recreation in Montana surpassing agriculture to emerge as the largest, most dynamic sector of the state's economy.

People like the phrase "Build it, and they will come." Here, though, the planet built the main attractions—the towering scenery, mountain-fresh air and water, plentiful wildlife, and other

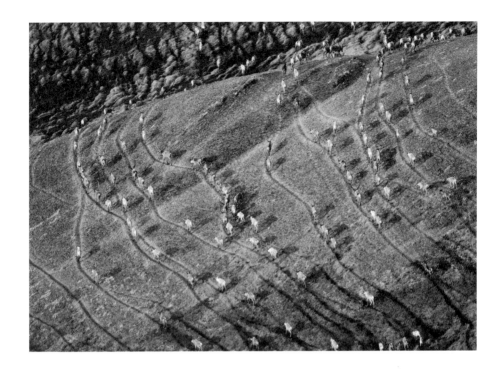

natural features that economists speak of as amenities. We need only to sustain them. The role of conservation as a strong stimulant to businesses is becoming a social and political game-changer. Residents of the Mountain West had grown accustomed to picking sides in the seemingly endless polarizing arguments between pro-industry representatives and conservationists, each camp labeling the other as the enemy of a brighter future. These days, more politicians and voters are looking toward the middle, intrigued by planning efforts that enlist a wide range of interest groups.

Cooperative decision-making certainly sounds good. In practice, finding common ground on environmental issues qualifies as one of the hardest challenges disparate groups can take on when they are more used to condemning opponents

A landscape furrowed by generations of caribou hoofs. Each year, the Porcupine herd migrates from wintering areas to the summer tundra of the arctic coastal plain, where calves are born, and back again, a round trip of about 800 miles.
FLORIAN SCHULZ

than listening to them. Can humans and wildlife truly prosper together over time? Of course they could. The underlying issue has always been whether people with different backgrounds and interests can work well enough with one another to make a better level of coexistence with nature possible. In a way, Y2Y is an experiment to find out how much better that level could be.

The answer isn't in plain view yet. But I've seen enough remarkable solutions forged to keep my expectations high. An early version from the Y2Y region involved a remote landscape of mountain ranges, lush river valleys, plains, waterfalls, lakes, hot springs, and big wildlife in northern British Columbia. Established as the Muskwa-Kechika Management Area in 1998 and enlarged in 2000, it is supervised by the provincial government with direction from a volunteer advisory council. The area is intended to serve as an example of what managers like to call "integrative and adaptive resource conservation." That means allowing logging in some areas and oil and gas development in others while treating still other portions as undisturbed parkland. It also means standing ready to revise the mix as environmental conditions, technologies, commodity markets, social priorities, or other influences change through the years. However, the prime directive, meant to stay constant, is to keep the area's overall wilderness character unimpaired and its native animals flourishing.

I traversed a long stretch of Muskwa-Kechika on a packhorse trip. The lead horse was ridden by Wayne Sawchuck, a trapper, former logger, experienced wrangler, and ardent conservationist. He was also a current advisory council member, and one of the people responsible for getting this landscape protected in the first place. My memories are of swimming glacier-fed rivers astride my mount and of jumping down and grabbing reins to help hold our group together each time we crossed paths with a grizzly. I recall, too, getting off to walk in front of my horse as we followed a ridgeline trail that Wayne said had been a major travel route for First Nations people since anyone could remember. I just felt I should be afoot there, stepping where so many generations had stepped before, because all the country in view looked as perfectly wild as it would have to someone on foot thousands of years earlier.

Will a person walking there a few hundred years from now be able to see and feel what I did? A few decades from now? The proportions of the landscape where various degrees of development activity are permitted will likely get rejiggered and tweaked as time goes on; that's the adaptive management provision. Sound problematic? No doubt, it will be complicated. Yet the Muskwa-Kechika Management Area encompasses 16 million acres. That makes it bigger than the state of West Virginia and approaching the size of Ireland. There is room for missteps, room to repair them, and room for improvements. As long as Muskwa-Kechika's mandate to prioritize wilderness qualities and wildlife needs holds up, the expanse will play a prominent role in the progress of the Y2Y Initiative toward its goal. It will continue to turn wishful thinking into that much more of a large-landscape conservation reality that has become a model for big, transboundary conservation projects elsewhere in the world.

Early in 2017, the government of Alberta established 63,000-acre Castle Provincial Park along the Rockies' eastern slope. Among the newest reserves in the Y2Y ecoregion, it connects to the northern end of Castle Wildland Provincial Park, a more strictly protected area that was expanded in size to 197,000 acres the same year. That enlarged reserve in turn connects to the northern end of 125,000-acre Waterton Lakes National Park. Waterton is buffered by conservation easements on ranchlands along its eastern boundary and connects as well to the northeastern border of Montana's million-acre Glacier National Park. Glacier's eastern boundary is the Blackfeet Reservation, where members of the Blackfeet Nation are working to restore bison. Glacier Park also adjoins the northern edge of the 287,000-acre Great Bear Wilderness in Montana's Flathead National Forest, which adjoins the million-acre Bob Marshall Wilderness, whose eastern side borders more than a quarter-million acres of prairie-edge ranchlands lately placed under conservation easements.

Look at that. Done. Next?

· · ·

John Muir, the late nineteenth- and early twentieth-century naturalist who led the push to create Yosemite National Park and preserve other wildlands, said, "When one tugs at a single thing in nature, he finds it connected to the rest of the world." Centuries before that, Leonardo da Vinci had simply advised, "Learn to see. Realize that everything connects to everything else."

We now know that, like every multicellular being, we humans rely upon a spectrum of material connections with other organisms that include actual mergers—our symbioses. Benefits also arise from our emotional connections to other beings and to the places where we dwell. As the effects of forest-bathing suggest, we also have bonds with natural settings that we may not even be conscious of but that strongly influence our physiology anyway. Whatever unravels our sense of connectedness and belonging can put a strain on our well-being as surely as out-of-balance ecosystems can impair our body's health. Wholeness in people, both mental and physical, is inextricably bound up with the wholeness of our environment.

To say it once more: humans are part of nature, and nature is part of humankind, and in this truth we discover our greater selves. And yet right now, modern civilization seems intent on extracting all the natural resources it can at the expense of the rest of the biosphere. The results of this frenzy are foreboding, to say the least. But that can change if the relationship between our present-day cultures and the natural world becomes more like a true mutualism—the sort of symbiosis in which each partner gains obvious sustained benefits from what the other is doing. Is there any reason not to move in that direction?

To keep nature truly protected, keep nature connected. Do the same to enrich the quality of human life. The proof is out there trotting, prowling, climbing, calling, courting—and backpacking and wildlife-viewing—along the continent's crest as I write. But don't take my word for Y2Y's virtues; I live in this ecoregion and love the landscape too much to be unbiased. Look into the Y2Y Initiative and judge for yourself. I'll offer the same advice as I would about Island Conservation: if you decide not to support it in some way, keep looking until you find a better program for strengthening nature and human nature together and put your spirit into making that one work. In the Anthropocene, the living planet needs all the solutions we're able to muster today, and the people who inherit the place from us are going to need them even more. Hold a meeting of holobionts, by which I mean sit down and have yourself a bowl of strawberries, and think it over.

And then do something!

NEXT SPREAD

Humpback whales in southeast Alaska surround a herring school and one humpback then circles beneath them blowing streams of rising bubbles. The whales then drive the startled fish caught within this bubble net upward and all surface together to gulp a meal.
PAUL SOUDERS/ GETTY IMAGES

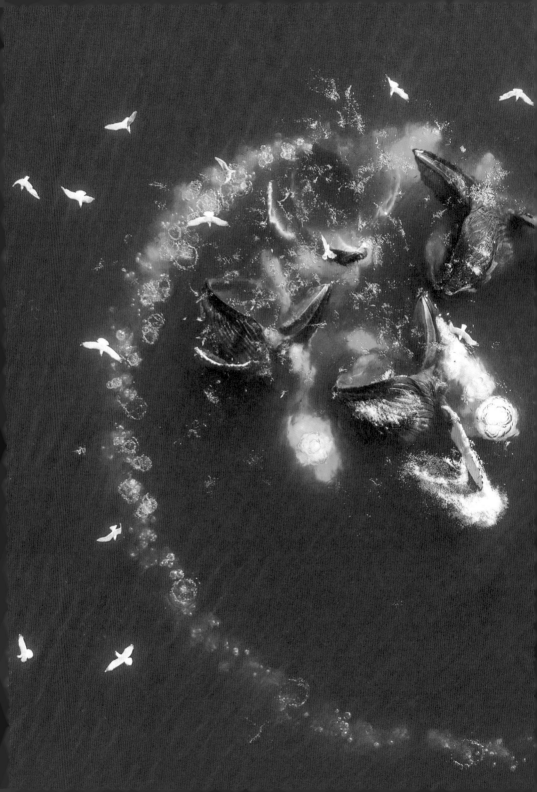

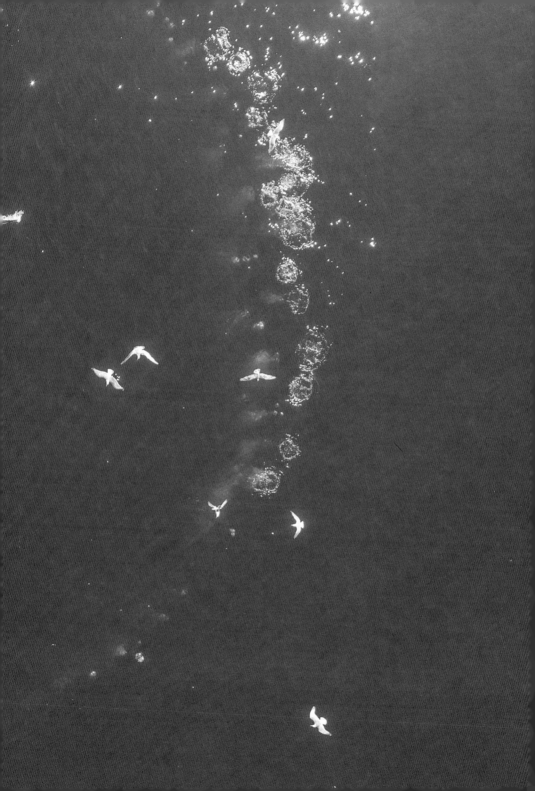

Note to (Greater) Self

It's a little strange, but I hold vivid memories of three settings—bivouacked deep in the Gobi Desert, sailing far out at sea, and camped 16,000 feet up in a range of the Himalaya—where I was actually grateful if I had to get up to pee in the small hours. It meant another opportunity to gaze into an exceptionally clear, boundless night sky awash in stars. Taking a sudden dunk into the universe while too groggy to drag along any preconceptions always left me standing there—a little open-mouthed speck of life within a glittering immensity—marveling that I should exist. But after a while I would begin to wonder who and what else might be out there. I'm guessing you've done that too. Maybe you've even imagined a creature on some distant world looking up into the heavens and wondering about the same thing.

Of course it is possible that, as some believe, Earth is the only planet with just the right conditions to support living things.

On the other hand, given countless planets circling countless suns in countless galaxies, the statistical probability that life has arisen just one time in one place is low. Wherever astronomers point their spectroscopes among the stars, they detect hydrogen, carbon, nitrogen, and organic molecules made from combinations of those elements. Organic compounds including amino acids (the basic components of proteins), nucleobases (the type of nitrogen compounds that go into the formation of nucleic acids), phosphate, and various sugars have been detected inside fragments of comets and meteors that have landed on Earth. Late in 2019, a paper in the *Proceedings of the National Academy of Sciences* reported the discovery of another sugar, ribose, in meteorites for the first time. This was exciting because ribose is the base ingredient of the genetic messenger molecule RNA, ribonucleic acid, in all living cells.

A growing number of experts believe that if the extraterrestrial fireballs pelting our planet through the ages didn't actually seed it with microbes from somewhere else (a possibility known as the panspermia theory) they at least delivered the

This stony meteorite sample contains traces of ribose, a simple sugar, also present as a key component of the genetic molecules RNA (ribonucleic acid) and DNA (deoxyribonucleic acid) in life here on Earth. YOSHIHIRO FURUKAWA

Tardigrades—also called water bears—are barely the size of a dust mite. There are at least 1,300 species of them. They can withstand extremes of heat, cold, drying, poisoning, and radiation. What scientists don't know yet is exactly what kind of animals they are. EYE OF SCIENCE/SCIENCE SOURCE

chemical building blocks of DNA and RNA—of self-replicating life. Nobody can yet say whether Earth is the sole planet with life or not. Nevertheless, I can confidently answer the question, Do you think we are alone in the universe?

No way.

How can I be so sure?

Because we exist within a pageant of different kinds of beings. Some grow from tiny seeds to tower so high they shade us from the sun. Some scuttle over the ground on dozens of legs, and some ride dust particles in the jet stream. And every one of them, great and small, indescribably beautiful or weirder-looking than any alien found in science fiction books or movies, not only keeps us company as we wheel through the heavens but also happens to be a relative. We couldn't be alone if we tried.

"Yeah, yeah. But I was talking about the chance that we'll be visited by other intelligent life forms one day."

Have you ever had a wild bird alight to eat out of your hand? Haven't you owned a cat or dog? Did you not notice how they train you to respond to some of their postures and actions as you work to train them? A seeing-eye dog assisting a blind person involves sophisticated communication between two different kinds of sentient beings with considerable learning abilities, doesn't it? People have been carrying on spoken conversations with African gray parrots and talking in a form of sign language with apes for decades. Captive dolphins trained to push buttons with different symbols on them in a certain sequence sometimes purposefully make all the wrong choices because they are so smart and so damn bored with the tests.

Suppose we do get visited by alien life forms. What if we find their appearance hideous and they consider us equally repulsive (assuming they even have emotions)? What if they believe their intellect to be the true measure of smarts and classify us as not very bright by comparison? What if instead of bestowing warp-speed multidimensional computers and miraculous medical cures upon us, they turn out to be colonists? We'd have to hope they relate to us far better than our own civilizations treated the Indigenous people they "discovered" and far better than we've treated most other native Earthlings. Suppose the alien leaders simply decide we're not worth the bother of keeping around as they develop the planet to their liking? In that case, our only chance is that the starship's crew includes some persuasive conservationists ... .

Then again, let's suppose that the folks who believe the rest of the universe is devoid of life are right, or that life does exist someplace else in the cosmos, but it is light years away and untold human generations will come and go before we contact it. Doesn't that make each variety of being with us now on the Earth infinitely more interesting and infinitely more precious?

Why, then, are we behaving in ways that before this century is over may extinguish a third or more of the planet's visible species? A third or more of all the unique expressions of life in the universe that we're aware of to date? A third or more of our genetic kin, our greater selves? The toll could include more than half the species of large fauna, the creatures that have the strongest influence on our art, stories, symbols, and affections. It looks as though we're going to have to decide, quickly, how important wild species and the fellowship, insights, and inspiration they offer are. Be sure to include all the physical and chemical inventions stored in their genes and available for us to decode, learn, and borrow from to improve our lives. Obliterating so much of the wonder and potential knowledge that this living world holds is anything but a sign of wisdom. Our hypothetical alien visitors might not be too far wrong if they wrote us off as clever critters but still far from genuinely intelligent.

Maybe we'll somehow escape the worst environmental consequences of the forces we've set in motion that are degrading our own living quarters while driving other life forms to extinction. Perhaps our descendants will find ways to prosper in stripped-down ecosystems consisting mainly of microbes and domesticated plants and animals in the future. Perhaps not. Either way, for a species that arose among a profusion of other life forms in wild settings that still kindle a deep-rooted sense of belonging, existence in a world with ever-dwindling alternatives to being among crowds of other humans in artificial surroundings doesn't seem like a very fulfilling destiny. On the contrary, it seems needlessly confining.

Being one with nature sounds like an aspiration. It really isn't, because we already are. Nature remains omnipresent within us. That is our starting point. It follows that the greater the share of fellow Earthlings and vibrant ecosystems we usher into the future along with us, the wider the range of possibilities we will discover awaiting us there.

NEXT SPREAD

The aquanaut and the astronaut: the planktonic larva of a brittle star and Bruce McCandless II, making the first untethered space-walk, February 3, 1984. Different as they might seem in some respects, both of these life forms are free-floating and both are made from the very same stuff: water and stardust.
WIM VAN EGMOND AND NASA

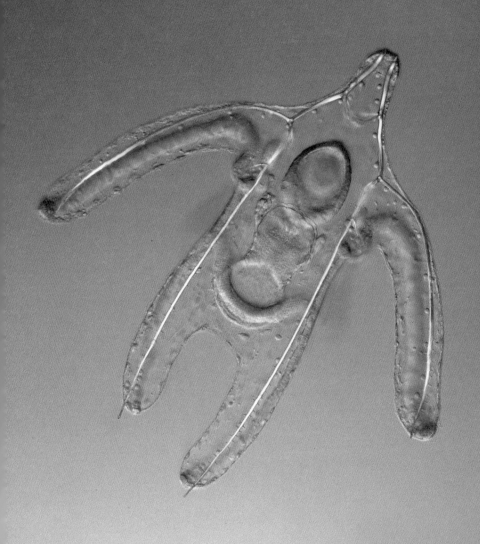

ENDNOTES

Prologue

1 D. E. Martinez, "Mortality Patterns Suggest Lack of Senescence in Hydra," *Experimental Gerontology* 33, no. 3 (May 1998): 217–25.

{ *The immortal jellyfish.* }

2 Douglas Chadwick, *A Beast the Color of Winter: The Mountain Goat Observed* (Lincoln: Bison Books/University of Nebraska Press, 2002).

Chapter 1
I'm at Least Four-Fifths Grizzly Bear

1 "Genes Are Us. And Them," https://doi: 10.1016/S1532-0464(02)00506-3.

2 Liping Wei et al., "Comparative Genomics Approaches to Study Organism Similarities and Differences," *Journal of Biomedical Informatics* 35, no. 2 (April 2002): 142–50, https://doi. org/10.1016/S1532-0464(02)00506-3.

3 Lydia Ramsey and Samantha Lee, "Humans Share Almost All of Our DNA with Cats, Cattle and Mice," *Independent*, April 6, 2018, https://www.independent. co.uk/news/science/human-dna-share-cats-cattle-mice-same-genetics-code-a8292111.html.

4 Kelly A. Frazer et al., "Cross-Species Sequence Comparisons: A Review of Methods and Available Resources," *Genome Research* 13, no. 1 (January 1, 2003): 1–12, https://doi:10.1101/gr.222003.

5 ResearchGate, https://doi:10.13140/ RG.2.1.3982.7684.

{ *Includes a list of twenty-seven publications, notably "Conservation of Grizzly Bear Populations and Habitat in the Northern Great Bear Rainforest," September 2015.* }

Chapter 2
Ka-Boom

1 Camilo Mora et al., "How Many Species Are There on Earth and in the Ocean?" *PLOS Biology*, August 23, 2011, https:// doi:10.1371/journal.pbio.1001127.

2 International Union for the Conservation of Nature, "IUCN Red List of Threatened Species," IUCN.org, https://www.iucn. org/resources/conservation-tools/ iucn-red-list-threatened-species.

{ *The International Union for the Conservation of Nature keeps official track of the status of plant, fungi, and animal species around the globe.* }

3 Sacha Vignieri et al., eds., "Vanishing Fauna," special issue, *Science* 345, no. 6195 (July 25, 2014): 392–95, https://www. sciencemag.org/site/special/vanishing/ index.xhtml?_ga=1.172413478.429831163.1 471029002.

4 https://www.sciencedirect.com/science/ article/pii/S2351989417300252#b78.

5 Bill Chappell and Nathan Rott, "1 Million Animal and Plant Species Are at Risk of Extinction, U.N. Report Says," *All Things Considered*, NPR, May 6, 2019, https:// www.npr.org/2019/05/06/720654249/1-million-animal-and-plant-species-face-extinction-risk-u-n-report-says.

6 Sophie Lewis, "Animal Populations Worldwide Have Declined by Nearly 70% in Just 50 Years, New Report Says," *CBS News*, September 10, 2020, https://www.cbsnews.com/news/endan-gered-species-animal-population-de-cline-world-wildlife-fund-new-report/.

7 Jonathan Watts, "Human Society under Urgent Threat from Loss of Earth's Natural Life," *Guardian*, May 6, 2019, https://www.theguardian.com/ environment/2019/may/06/human-soci-ety-under-urgent-threat-loss-earth-natu-ral-life-un-report.

8 Kew Royal Botanic Gardens, *State of the World's Plants and Fungi* (London: Kew Royal Botanic Gardens, 2020), https:// www.kew.org/sites/default/files/2020-09/ Kew%20State%20of%20the%20Worlds%20 Plants%20and%20Fungi.pdf.

{ *This report is distilled from detailed scientific papers and lists that have been made available in New Phytologist* }

Foundation, "Protecting and Sustainably Using the World's Plants and Fungi," special issue, *Plants, People, Planet* 2, no. 5 (September 2020): 367–579, https://nph.onlinelibrary.wiley.com/toc/25722611/2020/2/5. }

9   Sandra Diaz et al., *Summary for Policymakers of the Global Assessment Report on Biodiversity and Ecosystem Services*, unedited advance version (Bonn, Germany: Intergovernmental Science-Policy Platform on Biodiversity and Ecosystem Services, May 2019), https://assets.documentcloud.org/documents/5989433/IPBES-Global-Assessment-Summary-for-Policymakers.pdf.

10 Drew Kann, "The 'Ecological Foundations of Society' Are in Peril, a Massive UN Report Warns," CNN Health, March 13, 2019, https://www.cnn.com/2019/03/13/health/un-global-environment-outlook-report/index.html.

11 Damian Carrington, "World on Track to Lose Two-Thirds of Wild Animals by 2020, Major Report Warns," *Guardian*, October 26, 2016, https://www.theguardian.com/environment/2016/oct/27/world-on-track-to-lose-two-thirds-of-wild-animals-by-2020-major-report-warns.

12 Kenneth V. Rosenberg et al., "Decline of the North American Avifauna," *Science* 366, no. 6461 (October 4, 2019): 120–24, https://doi: 10.1126/science.aaw1313.

13 *Evolution*, PBS, https://www.pbs.org/wgbh/evolution/library/03/2/1_032_04.html.

    { A good explanation of the background-level extinctions throughout Earth's history. }

14 Helen Briggs, "Size Matters When It Comes to Extinction News," *BBC News*, September 19, 2017, https://www.bbc.com/news/science-environment-41279470.

    { Helen Briggs's story about the findings of international researchers that link larger body size with a higher risk of extinction in the modern environment. }

15 Center for Biological Diversity, "New Study Warns of Dire Human Impacts if Wildlife Extinction Crisis Continues," press release, June 1, 2020, https://biologicaldiversity.org/w/news/press-releases/new-study-warns-dire-human-impacts-if-wildlife-extinction-crisis-continues-2020-06-01/.

16 Francisco Sánchez-Bayo and Kris A. G. Wyckhuys, "Worldwide Decline of the Entomofauna: A Review of Its Drivers," *Biological Conservation* 232 (April 2019): 8–27, https://www.sciencedirect.com/science/article/pii/S0006320718313636.

17 Elizabeth Kolbert, *The Sixth Great Extinction: An Unnatural History* (New York: Henry Holt, 2014).

18 https://resiliencesystem.org/2050-there-will-be-more-plastic-fish-world%E2%80%99s-oceans-study-says.

    { Summarizes part of an extensive World Economic Forum report on the current and projected future use of plastics, "The New Plastics Economy, Rethinking the Future of Plastics," January 2016, http://www3.weforum.org/docs/WEF_The_New_Plastics_Economy.pdf. }

19 Matt Simon, "Plastic Rain Is the New Acid Rain," *Wired*, June 11, 2020, https://www.wired.com/story/plastic-rain-is-the-new-acid-rain/.

20 S. Allen et al., "Atmospheric Transport and Deposition of Microplastics in a Remote Mountain Catchment," *Nature Geoscience* 12 (2019): 339–44, https://doi:10.1038/s41561-019-0335-5.

21 Yuval Noah Harari, *A Brief History of Humankind* (New York: Harper Collins, 2015).

22 R. E. A. Almond, M. Grooten, and T. Petersen, eds., *Living Planet Report 2020—Bending the Curve of Biodiversity Loss* (Gland, Switzerland: WWF, 2020), https://www.wwf.org.uk/sites/default/files/2020-09/LPR20_Full_report.pdf.

Chapter 3
The Living Planet Quick Reference
Guide

1   Gary Kaiser, "1.3 Classification—The Three Domain System," LibreTexts. org, updated January 3, 2021, https:// bio.libretexts.org/Bookshelves/ Microbiology/Book%3A_Microbiology_ (Kaiser)/Unit_1%3A_Introduction_to_ Microbiology_and_Prokaryotic_Cell_ Anatomy/1%3A_Fundamentals_of_ Microbiology/1.3%3A_Classification_-_ The_Three_Domain_System.

{ A long citation but a short, quick general overview of the classification of living things. }

2   John Rennie and Lucy Reading-Ikkanda, "Seeing the Beautiful Intelligence of Microbes," *Quanta Magazine,* November 13, 2017, https://www.quantamagazine. org/the-beautiful-intelligence-of-bacteria-and-other-microbes-20171113/.

3   Luis Villazon, "How Long Does a Bacterium Live?" *Q&As, Science Focus Magazine,* https://www. sciencefocus.com/nature/ how-long-does-a-bacterium-live/.

4   Elaine R. Ingham, *The Living Soil: Bacteria* (Washington, DC: USDA Natural Resources Conservation Service/ Soils), https://www.nrcs.usda.gov/wps/ portal/nrcs/detailfull/soils/health/ biology/?cid=nrcs142p2_053862.

5   *Wikipedia,* "Choanoflagellate," last modified February 10, 2021, https://en.wikipedia.org/wiki/Choanoflagellate.

{ A good example of an organism that blurs the boundary between protist, plant, and animal. }

6   Katia Moskvitch, "Slime Molds Remember—but Do They Learn?," *Wired,* July 14, 2018, https://www.wired.com/story/ slime-molds-rememberbut-do-they-learn/.

7   DecodingScience Staff, "The Blob Attacks: Gooey Slime Mold Is an Example of Leaderless Motion,"

DecodedScience.org, https:// decodedscience.org/the-blob-attacks-gooey-slime-mold-is-an-exampleof-leaderless-motion/.

8   Elizabeth Pennisi, "The Momentous Transition to Multicellular Life May Not Have Been So Hard After All," *Science,* June 28, 2018, https://www.sciencemag. org/news/2018/06/momentous-transition-multicellular-life-may-not-havebeen-so-hard-after-all.

{ Possible explanations and estimated dates for the origin of multicellular organisms. }

9   Ed Yong, "The Unique Merger That Made You (and Ewe, and Yew)," *Nautilus,* February 6, 2014, http://nautil.us/ issue/10/mergers--acquisitions/theunique-merger-that-made-you-and-eweand-yew.

{ The symbiotic bacteria within all eukaryote cells. }

10   Roberto Kolter and Stanley Maloy, eds., *Microbes and Evolution: The World That Darwin Never Saw* (Washington, DC: ASM Press, 2012), https:// doi:10.1128/9781555818470.ch0.

11   Olena Shmahalo, "Cells Talk in a Language That Looks Like Viruses," *Quanta Magazine,* updated May 4, 2018, https://www.quantamagazine.org/ cells-talk-in-a-language-that-looks-likeviruses-20180502/.

{ Another way in which viruses may influence living systems and evolution. }

12   Michael Skinner, "Unified Theory of Evolution," *Aeon,* November 9, 2016, https://getpocket.com/explore/item/ unified-theory-of-evolution?utm_ source=pocket-newtab.

13   David Quammen, *The Tangled Tree: A Radical New History of Life* (New York: Simon & Schuster, 2018).

14   Sarah C. P. Williams, "Humans May Harbor More than 100 Genes from Other Organisms," *Science,* March 12,

2015, https://www.sciencemag.org/news/2015/03/humans-may-harbor-more-100-genes-other-organisms.

15 James Gorman, "A Virus in Koala DNA Shows Evolution in Action," *New York Times*, October 10, 2019, https://www.nytimes.com/2019/10/10/science/koala-retrovirus-evolution.html.

16 Tobias Rees, "From the Anthropocene to the Microbiocene," *NOĒMA Magazine*, June 10, 2020, https://www.noemamag.com/from-the-anthropocene-to-the-microbiocene/.

    { A timely perspective on COVID and society's understanding of nature. }

Chapter 5
Health Coverage for Primates

1 Neal Buccino and Rutgers University, "City Apartments or Jungle Huts: What Chemicals and Microbes Lurk Inside?" *ScienceDaily*, November 4, 2019, https://www.sciencedaily.com/releases/2019/11/191104112904.htm.

2 Kathleen Doheny, "Forest Bathing, Nature Time Are Hot Health Advice," *WebMD*, June 11, 2019, https://www.webmd.com/balance/news/20190611/forest-bathing-nature-time-hot-health-advice.

3 Chris Colin, "What Is 'Forest-Bathing'—and Can It Make You Healthier?" *Outside Magazine* 22 (August 2018), https://www.theguardian.com/us-news/2018/aug/22/forest-bathing-california-shinrin-yoku-nature-therapy.

4 Mel Greaves, "A Causal Mechanism for Childhood Acute Lymphoblastic Leukaemia," *Nature Reviews Cancer* 18 (2018): 471–84, https://www.nature.com/articles/s41568-018-0015-6.

5 World Health Organization, "7 Million Premature Deaths Annually Linked to Air Pollution," news release, March 25, 2014, https://www.who.int/mediacentre/news/releases/2014/air-pollution/en/.

6 Jacqueline Howard, "The US Suicide Rate Is Up 33% Since 1999, Research Says," *CNN Health*, June 20, 2019, https://www.cnn.com/2019/06/20/health/suicide-rates-nchs-study/index.html.

7 Kate Baggaley, "City Life Damages Health in Ways We're Just Beginning to Understand," *Popular Science*, May 13, 2019, https://www.popsci.com/physical-surroundings-cities-mental-illness/.

    { Urban environmental stressors may influence rates of schizophrenia and depression. }

8 Melissa Hogenboom, "How Air Pollution Is Doing More than Killing Us," *BBC Future*, April 16, 2019, https://www.bbc.com/future/article/20190415-how-air-pollution-is-doing-more-than-killing-us.

    { The possible links to health, cognitive abilities, behavior, and crime. }

9 Jen Christensen, "US Life Expectancy Is Still on the Decline. Here's Why," *CNN Health*, November 26, 2019, https://www.cnn.com/2019/11/26/health/us-life-expectancy-decline-study/index.html.

10 Gregory N. Bratman et al., "Nature Experience Reduces Rumination and Subgenual Prefrontal Cortex Activation," in *Proceedings of the National Academy of Sciences*, July 14, 2015, https://doi.org/10.1073/pnas.1510459112.

Chapters 6 and 7
Elephants and Excavations and Daydreaming at the Fair

1 Cassie Freund, "Biodiversity Doesn't Just Arise out of Healthy Ecosystems. It Helps Create Them," *Massive Science*, October 12, 2017, https://massivesci.com/articles/biodiversity-environment-regulation-resilience.

2 Tamanna Kalaïm, "What Role Do Elephants Play in Ecosystems?" *ScienceABC*, updated October 15, 2020, https://www.scienceabc.com/nature/animals/what-role-do-elephants-play-in-ecosystems.html.

    { What makes these giants a keystone species within ecosystems. }

3 World Wildlife Magazine, "The Status of African Elephants *Loxodonta Africana*," *World Wildlife Magazine*, Winter 2018, https://www.worldwildlife.org/magazine/issues/winter-2018/articles/the-status-of-african-elephants.

4 Sinalo Malindie, Daryl Codron, and Falko Buschke, "Niche Partitioning in African Antelopes," Society for Conservation Biology, 2020, https://conbio.org/groups/sections/africa/act/niche-partitioning-in-african-antelopes.

5 Kevin R. Theis, Thomas M. Schmidt, and Kay E. Holekamp, "Evidence for a Bacterial Mechanism for Group-Specific Social Odors among Hyenas," *Scientific Reports* 2 (August 30, 2012): 615, https://doi:10.1038/srep00615.

6 Marcia González-Teuber, Martin Kaltenpoth, and Wilhelm Boland, "Mutualistic Ants as an Indirect Defence against Leaf Pathogens," *New Phytologist*, January 6, 2014, https://doi:10.1111/nph.12664.

{*For a less technical article drawn from this material, see Max Planck Institute for Chemical Ecology, "Ants Protect Acacia Plants against Pathogens," ScienceDaily, January 15, 2014, https://www.sciencedaily.com/releases/2014/01/140115113243.htm.*}

7 Carl Zimmer, "These Ants Use Germ-Killers, and They're Better than Ours," *New York Times*, September 26, 2019, https://www.nytimes.com/2019/09/26/science/ants-fungus-antibiotic-resistance.html.

{*Another example of ants using microbe partners to discourage pathogens in an equatorial ecosystem.*}

8 P. Bonfante and A. Genre, "Mechanisms Underlying Beneficial Plant-Fungus Interactions in Mycorrhizal Symbiosis," *Nature Communications* 1, no. 48 (2010), https://doi.org/10.1038/ncomms1046.

9 Panos Sapountzis et al., "Potential for Nitrogen Fixation in the Fungus-Growing Termite Symbiosis," *Frontiers in Microbiology* 7 (December 2016): e261126, https://doi:10.3389/fmicb.2016.01993.

10 Jennifer Frazer, "Root Fungi Can Turn Pine Trees into Carnivores—or at Least Accomplices," *The Artful Amoeba* (blog), *Scientific American*, May 12, 2015, https://blogs.scientificamerican.com/artful-amoeba/root-fungi-can-turn-pine-trees-into-carnivores-8212-or-at-least-accomplices/.

11 UC Museum of Paleontology, "Introduction to the Nematoda," https://ucmp.berkeley.edu/phyla/ecdysozoa/nematoda.html.

12 Elaine R. Ingham et al., *Soil Biology Primer* (Washington, DC: Natural Resources Conservation Service, https://www.nrcs.usda.gov/wps/portal/nrcs/detailfull/soils/health/biology/?cid=nrcs142p2_053860.

{*A primer on the numbers and ecological roles of soil inhabitants from bacteria and fungi to springtails and mites, from the US Department of Agriculture's Natural Resources Conservation Service.*}

13 Ed Yong, "The Microbes That Supercharge Termite Guts," *Atlantic*, October 16, 2017, https://www.theatlantic.com/science/archive/2017/10/termites-contain-multitudes/543015/.

14 Jonathan Watts, "Scientists Identify Vast Underground Ecosystem Containing Billions of Micro-Organisms," *Guardian*, December 10, 2018, https://www.theguardian.com/science/2018/dec/10/tread-softly-because-you-tread-on-23bn-tonnes-of-micro-organisms.

15 Nic Fleming, "Which Life Form Dominates Earth?" *BBC–Earth*, February 10, 2015, http://www.bbc.com/earth/story/20150211-whats-the-most-dominant-life-form.

{*An interesting overview taking in categories from bacteria to plants and insects.*}

Chapters 8 and 9
Rescue at Sea, Parts 1 and 2

1 Sascha K. Hooker and Robin W. Baird, "Deep-Diving Behavior of the Northern Bottlenose Whale, *Hyperoodon ampullatus* (Cetacea: Ziphiidae)," in *Proceedings of the Royal Society of London B* 266 (1999): 671–76, https://www.cascadiaresearch.org/files/Projects/Hawaii/bnw-dive.pdf.

2 *Wikipedia*, "Dwarf Elephant," last modified February 18, 2021, https://en.wikipedia.org/wiki/Dwarf_elephant.

   { Overview of small elephants, mastodons, and mammoths on islands. }

3 "Spotlight on Island Biogeography," *Bagheera's Lair* (blog), *Endangered Species Journalist*, 2021, https://www.bagheera.com/spotlight-on-island-biogeography/.

   { Why island-dwelling species are both especially subject to evolutionary change and especially vulnerable to extinction. }

4 Virginia Morell, "Why Did New Zealand's Moas Go Extinct?" *Science*, March 17, 2014, https://www.sciencemag.org/news/2014/03/why-did-new-zealands-moas-go-extinct.

5 Lorraine Boissoneault, "A New Genetic Study Suggests Modern Flores Island Pygmies and Ancient Hobbits Are Unrelated," *Smithsonian Magazine*, August 2, 2018, https://www.smithsonianmag.com/science-nature/new-genetic-study-suggests-modern-flores-island-pygmies-and-ancient-hobbits-are-unrelated-180969858/.

6 Sally Esposito, "Want to Save 41 Percent of the Planet's Highly Threatened Vertebrates? Work on Islands," University of California, Santa Cruz Newscenter, October 25, 2017, https://news.ucsc.edu/2017/10/island-species.html.

7 James C. Russell and Nick D. Holmes, "Tropical Island Conservation: Rat Eradication for Species Recovery," special issue, *Biological Conservation* 185 (May 2015): 1–7, https://www.sciencedirect.com/science/article/abs/pii/S0006320715000117.

8 Tim Stephens, "From Wind to Whales: Understanding an Ecosystem," *University of California, Santa Cruz Review*, Summer 2002, https://review.ucsc.edu/summer-02/wind2whales.html.

   { A nontechnical description of researcher Don Croll's research on blue whales and krill ecology. }

9 Andrew S. Wright, "Preventing Extinctions," *National Observer*, April 25, 2020, https://www.nationalobserver.com/2020/04/30/preventing-extinctions.

   { Reporting on rat removal by Island Conservation on the Palmyra Atoll, with intriguing speculations on patterns of evolution. }

10 Dena R. Spatz et al., "Globally Threatened Vertebrates on Islands with Invasive Species," *Science Advances* 3, no. 10 (October 2017), https://doi:10.1126/sciadv.1603080.

11 Emily Heber, "Science Has Spoken: Coral Reefs Thrive by Rat-Free Islands," Island Conservation online, July 12, 2018, https://www.islandconservation.org/science-spoken-restoring-islands-helps-save-coral-reef-biodiversity/.

12 Victoria Gill, "Killing Rats Could Save Coral Reefs," *BBC News Science*, July 12, 2018, https://www.bbc.com/news/science-environment-44799420.

   { Additional information on the rat removal–coral reef rebound effect. }

13 Island Conservation, "Island Conservation Impact Report 2017–2018," https://www.islandconservation.org/report/2018/?utm_source=Island%20Conservation%20Newsletter&utm_campaign=3d-d38a057e-2017-2018%20Impact%20Report%20%28Donor%29&utm_medium=email&utm_term=0_778049eff2-3dd38a057e-127659613.

   { Summary report of projects. }

Chapters 10 and 11
Ode to a Strawberry and
Coda to a Strawberry

1   José M. Alvarez-Suarez et al., "One-Month Strawberry-Rich Anthocyanin Supplementation Ameliorates Cardiovascular Risk, Oxidative Stress Markers and Platelet Activation in Humans," *Journal of Nutritional Biochemistry* 25, no. 3 (2014): 289, https://doi:10.1016/j.jnutbio.2013.11.002.

2   Aedin Cassidy et al., "High Anthocyanin Intake Is Associated with a Reduced Risk of Myocardial Infarction in Young and Middle-Aged Women," *Circulation: Journal of the American Heart Association,* January 15, 2013, https://doi:10.1161/CIRCULATIONAHA.112.122408.

3   Sara Tulipani et al., "Strawberry Intake Increases Blood Fluid, Erythrocyte and Mononuclear Cell Defenses against Oxidative Challenge," *Food Chemistry* 156 (2014): 87, https://doi:10.1016/j.foodchem.2014.01.098.

4   Arthritis Foundation, "Best Fruits for Arthritis," https://www.arthritis.org/health-wellness/healthy-living/nutrition/healthy-eating/best-fruits-for-arthritis.

5   Gary Heiting, "Lutein and Zeaxanthin: Eye and Vision Benefits," All About Vision, December 2017, https://www.allaboutvision.com/nutrition/lutein.htm.

6   Valeria Todeschini et al., "Impact of Beneficial Microorganisms on Strawberry Growth, Fruit Production, Nutritional Quality, and Volatilome," *Frontiers in Plant Science* 9 (2018): 1611, https://doi:10.3389/fpls.2018.01611.

7   Adriana C. Flores-Gallegos and Erika Nava-Reyna, "Plant-Growth-Promoting Microbial Enzymes," chap. 30 in *Enzymes in Food Biotechnology: Production, Applications, and Future Prospects* (Cambridge, MA: Academic Press, 2019), 521–34.

8   Rudi Emerson de Lima Procópio et al., review article, "Antibiotics Produced by *Streptomyces*," *Brazilian Journal of Infectious Diseases* 16, no. 5 (September–October 2012): 466–71.

9   Andre Schiefner et al., "Structural Basis for the Enzymatic Formation of the Key Strawberry Flavor Compound 4-Hydroxy-2,5-dimethyl-3(2H)-furanone," *Journal of Biological Chemistry* 288, no. 23 (June 7, 2013): 16815–26, https://doi: 10.1074/jbc.M113.453852.

10 Constantina Nasopoulou et al., "Localization of Strawberry (*Fragaria x ananassa*) and *Methylobacterium extorquens* Genes of Strawberry Flavor Biosynthesis in Strawberry Tissue by In Situ Hybridization," *Journal of Plant Physiology* 171, no. 13 (August 15, 2014): 1099–105, https://doi:10.1016/j.jplph.2014.03.018.

11 University of Alberta news release, "Individual Lichens Can Have up to Three Fungi," *Science Daily*, January 17, 2019, https://www.sciencedaily.com/releases/2019/01/190117142055.htm.

    { A follow-up on Tony Spribille's original discovery. For technical details, see Veera Tuovinen et al., "Two Basidiomycete Fungi in the Cortex of Wolf Lichens," Current Biology 29, no. 3 (February 4, 2019): 476–83.E5, https://doi:10.1016/j.cub.2018.12.022. }

12 Bet Hölldobler and Edward O. Wilson, *The Superorganism: The Beauty, Elegance, and Strangeness of Insect Societies* (New York: W. W. Norton, 2008).

13 Joanna Klein, "How Ants Figured Out Farming Millions of Years Before Humans," *New York Times*, April 11, 2017, https://www.nytimes.com/2017/04/11/science/ant-fungus-farmers-evolution.html.

14 Douglas H. Chadwick, "Sisterhood of Weavers," *National Geographic Magazine*, May 2011, https://www.nationalgeographic.com/magazine/2011/05/weaver-ants/.

15 ScienceDirect, "Parthenogenesis," ScienceDirect.com, https://www.sciencedirect.com/topics/agri-cultural-and-biological-sciences/parthenogenesis.

Chapter 12
Crowboarding

1 Kristin Andrews, "Animal Cognition," in *Stanford Encyclopedia of Philosophy*, ed. Edward N. Zalta (Palo Alto, CA: Metaphysics Research Lab, Stanford University, Summer 2016), https://plato.stanford.edu/archives/sum2016/entries/cognition-animal.

 { A well-researched overview of animal mental abilities with extensive references for further reading. }

2 Suzana Herculano-Houzel, "The Remarkable, Yet Not Extraordinary, Human Brain as a Scaled-Up Primate Brain and Its Associated Cost," vol. VI, chap. 8, *Brain and Behavior*, in *In the Light of Evolution* (Washington, DC: The National Academies Press, 2013).

3 Jennifer Vonk and Michael J. Beran, "Bears 'Count' Too: Quantity Estimation and Comparison in Black Bears, *Ursus americanus*," *Animal Behavior* 84, no. 1 (July 2012): 231–38, https://doi.org/10.1016/j.anbehav.2012.05.001.

4 Jason G. Goldman, "The Average Bear is Smarter Than You Thought," *Scientific American* (blog), June 20, 2012, https://blogs.scientificamerican.com/thoughtful-animal/the-average-bear-is-smarter-than-you-thought/.

5 Volker Deecke, "Tool-Use in the Brown Bear *(Ursus arctos)*," *Animal Cognition* 15 (2012): 725–30, https://doi.org/10.1007/s10071-012-0475-0.

6 Peter Hess, "New Caledonian Crows Are Even Smarter and Scarier than We Thought," Inverse.com, June 28, 2018, https://www.inverse.com/article/46535-how-do-crows-make-tools.

7 Ross Andersen, "A Journey into the Animal Mind," *Atlantic*, March 2019, https://www.theatlantic.com/magazine/archive/2019/03/what-the-crow-knows/580726/.

8 Jeff Salzman, "Monkey Mind (and Other Kinds of Animal Intelligence)," *Daily Evolver Podcast*, https://www.dailyevolver.com/2017/09/monkey-mind-and-other-kinds-of-animal-intelligence/.

9 Kevin Laland, "Evolution Unleashed," *Aeon Newsletter*, https://aeon.co/essays/science-in-flux-is-a-revolution-brewing-in-evolutionary-theory.

10 Frans de Waal, *Mama's Last Hug: Animal Emotions and What They Tell Us about Ourselves* (New York: W. W. Norton, 2020).

11 Jason Daley, "Flowers Sweeten Up When They Hear Bees Buzzing," *Smithsonian Magazine*, January 18, 2019, https://www.smithsonianmag.com/smart-news/flowers-sweeten-when-they-hear-bees-buzzing-180971300/.

12 Daniel Kolitz, "Are Plants Conscious?" Gizmodo.com, May 28, 2018, https://gizmodo.com/are-plants-conscious-1826365668.

13 "Uncovering the Intelligence of Insects, an Interview with Lars Chittka," by Jeremy Hance, Mongabay.com, June 29, 2010, https://news.mongabay.com/2010/06/uncovering-the-intelligence-of-insects-an-interview-with-lars-chittka/.

14 Andrew D. Foote et al., "Genome-Culture Coevolution Promotes Rapid Divergence of Killer Whale Ecotypes," *Nature Communications*, May 31, 2016, https://www.nature.com/articles/ncomms11693.

Chapter 13
Why Y2Y?

1   Alan Buis, "Examining the Viability of Planting Trees to Help Mitigate Climate Change," NASA/Global Climate Change, November 7, 2019, https://climate.nasa.gov/news/2927/examining-the-viability-of-planting-trees-to-help-mitigate-climate-change/.

2   Carl Zimmer, "In Fragmented Forests, Rapid Mammal Extinctions," *New York Times*, September 26, 2013, https://www.nytimes.com/2013/09/27/science/in-fragmented-forests-rapid-mammal-extinctions.html?_r=0.

{ An example of the island extinction effect where mainland ecosystems become reduced to separate remnants. }

3   "The Effect of Area on Rainforest Species Richness," Mongabay.com, July 31, 2012, https://rainforests.mongabay.com/0303a.htm.

{ An early report on the Minimum Critical Size of Ecosystems Project experiment conducted in the Amazon forests of Brazil. }

4   Kim Stanley Robinson, "Empty Half the Earth of Its Humans. It's the Only Way to Save the Planet," *Guardian*, March 20, 2018, https://www.theguardian.com/cities/2018/mar/20/save-the-planet-half-earth-kim-stanley-robinson.

{ Despite the dramatic title, this is an explanation of the Half-Earth, or Nature Needs Half, initiative proposed by the noted ecologist E. O. Wilson to sustain the planet's biological diversity by clustering the human population rather than reducing its current numbers. }

5   E. O. Wilson, *Half-Earth: Our Planet's Fight for Life* (New York: W.W. Norton, 2016).

6   Center for Biological Diversity, "Human Population Growth and Extinction," https://www.biologicaldiversity.org/programs/population_and_sustainability/extinction/.

{ The graph showing the rapid growth rate of the modern human population and the parallel sharp increase in extinctions tells the story in one image. }

7   Eric Dinerstein et al., "An Ecoregion-Based Approach to Protecting Half the Terrestrial Realm," *BioScience* 67, no. 6 (June 2017): 534–45, https://doi.org/10.1093/biosci/bix014.

8   Harvey Locke, "The International Movement to Protect Half the World: Origins, Scientific Foundations, and Policy Implications," reference module in *Earth Systems and Environmental Sciences* (Amsterdam: Elsevier, October 30, 2018), https://doi:10.1016/B978-0-12-409548-9.10868-1.

9   Harvey Locke, "Nature Needs Half: A Necessary and Hopeful Agenda for Protected Areas," *Parks* 19, no. 2 (November 2013), https://parksjournal.com/wp-content/uploads/2013/11/PARKS-19.2-Locke-10.2305IUCN.CH_.2013.PARKS-19-2.HL_.en_.pdf.

10 David Western, John Waithaka, and John Kamanga, "Finding Space for Wildlife Beyond National Parks and Reducing Conflict through Community-Based Conservation: The Kenya Experience," *Parks* 21, no. 1 (March 2015): 51–62.

11 Yellowstone to Yukon Conservation Initiative, "Shrinking Landscapes: Why Y2Y Works to Prevent Islands of Wildlife," *Y2Y* blog, https://y2y.net/blog/shrinking-landscapes-why-y2y-works-to-prevent-islands-of-wildlife/.

{ A graphic showing past and current megafauna distribution in North America that highlights the Yellowstone to Yukon ecoregion as the remaining stronghold. }

12 Andrea S. Laliberte and William J. Ripple, "Range Contractions of

North American Carnivores and Ungulates, "*BioScience* 54, no. 2 (February 2004): 123–38, https://doi.org/10.1641/0006-3568(2004)054[023:RCONAC]2.0.CO;2.

13 Santiago Saura et al., "Protected Areas in the World's Ecoregions: How Well Connected Are They?" *Ecological Indicators* 76 (2017): 144–58, http://doi.org/10.1016/j.ecolind.2016.12.047.

{ *Global maps showing percentage of protection and connectivity on the continents.* }

14 Jim Robbins, "Can Wildlife Corridors Heal Fragmented Landscapes?" *Yale Environment 360* (October 10, 2011), https://e360.yale.edu/features/ecological_corridors_connecting_fragmented_pockets_of_wildlife_habitat.

15 https://www.tomudall.senate.gov/news/press-releases/udall-beyer-introduce-wildlife-corridors-conservation-act-to-safeguard-americas-biodiversity, December 6, 2018.

16 Brett Prettyman, "Still Room to Roam? Effort to Raise Awareness of Development's Threat to Wildlife Movement Draws Support from Outdoor Gear Heavyweight Patagonia," Travel and Outdoors, *Salt Lake City Tribune*, March 27, 2011.

17 Yellowstone to Yukon Conservation Initiative, "Our Impact," https://y2y.net/work/impact/.

{ *Maps comparing the connection and protection of areas in 1993 to the conservation progress achieved by 2013.* }

18 Canadian Press, "Alberta Expands Castle Area Parks, Plans to Phase Out Off-Highway Vehicles," *CBC News*, January 20, 2017, https://www.cbc.ca/news/canada/calgary/alberta-expands-castle-area-parks-plans-to-phase-out-off-highway-vehicles-1.3945625.

19 Marne Haynes, "Montana Tops Nation in Outdoor Recreation Economy,"

Bozeman Daily Chronicle, October 5, 2019, https://www.bozemandailychronicle.com/opinions/guest_columnists/montana-tops-nation-in-outdoor-recreation-economy/article_cf1e33d9-1158-5d0d-aff2-4d43972fd0f8.html.

20 "Outdoor Recreation Now the Largest Sector of Montana's Economy," *Wild Word* blog, August 4, 2017, https://wildmontana.org/wild-word/outdoor-recreation-now-the-largest-sector-of-our-economy.

21 Tristan Scott, "Another Ascent for the Outdoor Economy," *Flathead Beacon*, October 9, 2019, https://flatheadbeacon.com/2019/10/09/another-ascent-outdoor-economy/.

Epilogue: Note to (Greater) Self

1 Yoshihiro Furukawa et al., "Extraterrestrial Ribose and Other Sugars in Primitive Meteorites," in *Proceedings of the National Academy of Sciences*, November 18, 2019, https://doi.org/10.1073.

NEXT SPREAD

A species of one-to two-inch-long, mostly transparent sea slugs commonly called sea angels. Despite their celestial name and appearance, they are dedicated predators and feed exclusively on the group of free-swimming sea snails known as sea butterflies.

TIM FLACH

INDEX

NEXT SPREAD

Lost in reflections at Salar de Uyuni. Located in southeast Bolivia, this is the world's largest salt flat, sprawling across more than 4,000 square miles at an elevation of 11,995 feet in the Andes Mountains.
FERDINANDO GEREMICCA

Being one with nature sounds like an aspiration. It really isn't, because we already are.